CAROL ANNE DAVIS was born in Scotland and now lives in southwest England. She left school at fifteen and was everything from an artist's model to an editorial assistant before going to university. Her Master of the Arts degree included Criminology and was followed by a postgraduate diploma in Adult and Community Education. A full-time writer since graduating, her non-fiction books include *Children Who Kill*, *Couples Who Kill* and *Women Who Kill*.

www.*carolannedavis*.co.uk

By Carol Anne Davis

Women Who Kill
Children Who Kill
Couples Who Kill
Doctors Who Kill

a&b

Doctors Who Kill

Profiles of lethal medics

CAROL ANNE DAVIS

Allison & Busby Limited
13 Charlotte Mews
London W1T 4EJ
www.allisonandbusby.com

Hardcover published in Great Britain in 2010.
This paperback edition published in 2011.

A CIP catalogue record for this book is available from
the British Library.

10 9 8 7 6 5 4 3 2 1

ISBN 978-0-7490-0884-0

Typeset in 10.5/14 pt Sabon by
Allison & Busby Ltd.

The paper used for this Allison & Busby publication
has been produced from trees that have been legally sourced
from well-managed and credibly certified forests.

Printed and bound in the UK by
CPI Bookmarque, Croydon, CR0 4TD

For Ian
1957 – 2009

Contents

Introduction

When I worked for Women's Aid in the mid-Eighties, I was told that some of the most vicious wife-beaters were doctors. The literature on abused women included a lengthy confessional from a woman who had frequently been beaten by her husband, a respected British village-based GP. She said that he was revered by his staff and patients and demanded that his home life be similarly deferential, with nothing ever out of place. If a few of the children's toys were lying around or the Sunday roast wasn't quite ready, he would become enraged. Though he would punch and kick her with seeming abandon, he took care to aim his blows at her body rather than her face.

The woman admitted that she'd remained in the marriage because of the lifestyle that his salary afforded them and her fear of being alone, but had finally left after twenty years of fear and anguish. Later, I read similar stories from other British GPs' wives, and, when I began to write true crime books, found that murderous American doctors and surgeons often had a similar history of perpetrating domestic violence. Many of them had been denied a fun-filled childhood, instead growing up in families where academic achievement was everything, whilst others had been mocked and beaten throughout their formative years.

Expanding on this theme, the first part of this book, Doctor in the House, profiles medics who have killed a family member or members. Most murdered their long-suffering spouses, but one female doctor attempted to murder all three of her children in an arson attack.

The second part looks at killers on the ward and is self-explanatory. Most of these murderers were desperate for attention, creating endless dramas both at home and in the hospitals where they worked. They were belatedly diagnosed with personality disorders, ranging from borderline to full-blown psychopathy. The majority were nurses, who commit most medical murders, a total of 45%. The other 55% is made up of doctors, surgeons and an array of workers in paramedical roles.

Other sections look at medics in the media, particularly intriguing cases which captured the public imagination, and paramedics who murdered their partners in order to enjoy the single life. Those of a weak disposition may want to avoid the Paper Masks section, though dental-phobics can safely read the Deadly Dentists segment as none of the surgeons killed within their surgeries.

The penultimate part, Unbridled Lust, examines those who killed their patients – or strangers – after raping or sexually assaulting them, and includes the profile of a medical technician turned serial killer who is currently on Death Row, whilst the final section examines typologies of medical killers.

PART ONE

DOCTOR IN THE HOUSE

Though the medics in this section had potentially fatal drugs at their disposal, most chose to dispatch their victims by using traditional weapons – guns and knives – or even their bare hands. Unstable and controlling in their personal relationships, when challenged or faced with excessive demands, they exploded into violence.

The first seven chapters profile doctors who murdered a close relative, usually a wife but sometimes two or more of their own children. The other four chapters in this section focus on less-qualified medics who also killed in a domestic environment. These, too, were particularly brutal crimes, with the female paramedics stabbing, strangling and bludgeoning their friends in a paroxysm of rage at real and imagined slights.

1 Dr Richard John Sharpe

With his exceptional IQ and myriad skills, this doctor could have been anything that he wanted to be. Instead, he gave in to his rage with ultimately fatal results.

A terrifying childhood

Richard John Sharpe was born on the 23rd August 1954 to housewife Laura and toolmaker Benjamin in Connecticut, USA. He was their third son and, a mere fifteen months later, they had a fourth child, a girl.

Benjamin Sharpe worked long hours but he also played hard, drinking too much and running up sizeable gambling debts. At home he was a tyrant, beating his children and telling them that they were no good. He endlessly criticised his timid wife, beat his sons and even threatened Richard with a gun. Benjamin's own father, a religious zealot with mental health problems who lived next door, committed suicide.

Early cross-dressing

Richard noticed that his sister, Laura, was the only member of the family who wasn't beaten. Keen to become like her, he began to wear her clothes. This soon became a daily occurrence and, when he was twelve, he used money from his paper round to buy a girlish outfit of his own. With his small, slender figure and long hair, he was able to pass as a female and often went into town dressed as one.

By his early teens, he'd started to square up to his father and sometimes got the better of the older man. He also fought his corner in the playground and was aggressive in the classroom and on the street. His violence was wide ranging and he hit his mother and sister and killed several of the family pets. However, at seventeen, he showed a different side to his nature when a new girl, Karen, arrived at his high school. He wooed the sixteen-year-old with flattery and long romantic phone calls and, within months, she was expecting his child.

Fatherhood and marriage

On the last day of May 1973, Richard became a father for the first time. The couple called the baby Shannon. Karen took the child home to her parents, whilst Richard continued living with his. Almost everyone who knew them was against the match as, by now, Richard had shown repeatedly that he could be cold and arrogant. Realising that he was too controlling, Karen began a relationship with another teenager and, when Richard found out, he slapped her, after which they made up. That September they married secretly and moved into a rented flat.

Domestic violence

A week into the marriage, Richard overslept, blamed his new wife and threw an alarm clock at her. The abuse continued and he worked hard to alienate her from her family and friends. He was studying for an engineering degree and she supported him by working double shifts as a care assistant whilst also going to college part-time to train as a nurse.

By the mid-Seventies he was taking her birth control pills in order to grow breasts – this made him look even more womanly. Richard said that he hoped the pills would relieve stress, but he remained abusive and began to beat and mock their little daughter Shannon on a regular basis so that she became terrified of him. In 1978, he received his engineering degree but immediately changed path and enrolled on a medical course. He also continued to hit Karen and, in August 1979, assaulted her in front of a police officer. He was arrested but the charges were later dropped. By now he felt invincible; he beat Karen harder, leaving her with concussion, two black eyes and a broken nose. When Shannon was ten, he treated her with equal cruelty, blackening both her eyes.

Karen's response was to keep her daughter out of school for two days, after which Richard told the ten-year-old to explain to her teacher that she had fallen downstairs. Ironically, children from middle- and upper-class homes such as the Sharpes' are less likely to be perceived as domestic violence victims so adults tend to believe them when they say that they've sustained accidental injuries.

Like most abusers, Richard was determined to terrorise his spouse into staying with him, warning that he'd kill her parents and siblings (whom Karen was very close to) if she left.

Affairs

In 1985, at the age of thirty-one, Richard graduated from medical school and did a research year at a Massachusetts hospital. He then became a resident at Harvard Medical School whilst Karen continued to work in a nursing home. He had several affairs during his residency and would later allege that Karen had one too. When chatting up a new woman, he often introduced the subject of cross-dressing and showed them photos of himself in a female wig, make-up and attire. With his fine features and slender physique, he looked more feminine than most transvestites and was upset when some of his new girlfriends were repulsed and ended the relationship.

In the summer of 1990, he completed his residency and secured a highly paid job with a biotech company as a cancer researcher. He also taught part-time at medical school and studied to become a dermatologist, soon setting up a successful dermatology practice. He was often aloof with his patients and relied on Karen, now working part-time as his receptionist, to smooth over any ill feeling. She made increasing allowances for his short temper – after all, he was working eighty hours a week.

Mental health problems

Eventually, something had to give and Richard was so overworked and stressed that he fell into a near-stupor. His GP suggested he needed therapy, and he went to see a psychiatrist who diagnosed him as having clinical depression and a personality disorder. She prescribed Xanax, and he briefly felt better, then began to have stomach pains, for which he used larger and larger doses of painkillers. He also drank to give himself false energy. One weekday in April 1991, he felt so ill that he came home during the day, only to find Karen in bed with another man. Karen's lover left, after which the couple had a fight which continued into the next morning, when he stabbed her several times in the forehead with a fork and she kneed him in the groin and bit his hand.

She and Shannon fled the house and Karen told his psychiatrist that she feared for her life. The psychiatrist phoned Richard and his speech was so slurred that she suspected he'd taken an overdose. She phoned for an ambulance and they took the by-now-unconscious doctor to hospital, where he was revived, evaluated and committed involuntarily to a psychiatric facility. When Karen visited, he threatened her, saying that he would kill her relatives unless she revised her statement, and she did just that, stating that he had never been violent. He was soon released.

Richard continued to self-medicate, abusing alcohol and using samples of several prescription tranquillisers. His mood remained volatile and, on a bad day, he'd keep patients waiting for hours, but on good days he wrote erudite scientific papers which were published in medical journals and earned him an international reputation as a skin specialist.

He continued to cross-dress and had all of his body hair removed. He also had plastic surgery to make his features even more feminine and liposuction to remove excess fat from his body. Karen took photos of him dressed as a woman and was tolerant of his increasing links to the transgender community. Dressing in female attire was supposed to make him feel more relaxed, but he was still so stressed that he worked out obsessively for six nights each week at the gym.

Further victims

Karen helped Richard out at the office whenever she had time, but he'd repay her by calling her names in front of his patients and partners. Chillingly, the Sharpes chose to bring two further children into this violent atmosphere: a son in 1992 (by then, Shannon had left home and gone to college) and a daughter in 1995. By the time their son went to school, he was exhibiting deep concern for his mother and didn't want to leave her alone with his father for fear of what the man would do.

In 1997, the unstable but extremely hard-working doctor became a millionaire. The following year, he moved into the business of laser hair removal, setting up over a dozen successful franchises. But, by 2000, he was being threatened with a lawsuit from a rival company. Rather than risk losing everything, he transferred his house and almost three million dollars into Karen's name; in the same time frame, she began another affair. He continued to call her names and belittle her in front of friends and family, telling her that she was ugly, fat and dumb.

The final straw came when Richard returned from an all-night party, still in female attire and make-up. Shocked that he would show this side of himself to his seven-year-old son, Karen said that she wanted a divorce. In February, she left with her two children and moved into a family suite at a hotel. Shortly afterwards, she met up with Richard at a lawyer's office to discuss his access rights to their younger children. Both youngsters burst into tears when told that they still had to see their dad.

Like most wife-beaters, Richard fell apart when his punchbag finally left him, crying hysterically and begging Karen to reconsider. When she refused to reconcile, he sacked her from his company but failed to get his house transferred back into his name. He continued to self-medicate, and was so dazed the following month that he fell downstairs and broke his pelvis. He was hospitalised and patched up before being sent home with strong painkillers, which he added to his already sizeable daily dose of antidepressants and alcohol.

A brief reunion

Within weeks of Richard's accident, Karen's affair began to break down and she phoned her husband and foolishly took him back. He was ecstatic. But after four days of his strange mood swings and angry outbursts, she ordered him to leave and continued with the divorce. Richard now began to stalk her, and, in mid-May 2000, she took a restraining order out against him. Enraged, he began to plan her death and set about procuring a gun.

The murder

On 14th July 2000, 45-year-old Richard spent the evening drinking. Meanwhile, Karen, 44, was enjoying a rare night of freedom, having hired a babysitter and gone out to dinner with friends, her brother and his girlfriend. Richard phoned her mobile repeatedly throughout the evening but she refused to answer. Shortly after 11 p.m., she made her way home with her relatives.

In the same time frame, Richard took his rifle and drove to her house. He asked the babysitter if Karen was home but, before the girl could answer, Karen herself appeared in the kitchen doorway. She told him that he shouldn't be there, and, in response, he raised his rifle and aimed it at her chest. She turned to flee and the .22 bullet ripped through her back, tearing into her lungs and severing her spinal cord. She collapsed and Richard walked calmly back to his car and drove away.

The children had been woken by the noise and their son, now aged seven, started asking if his father had hurt his mother. Karen's brother, who had returned home with Karen after the meal, acted quickly to stem the blood and phone the emergency services, but she was beyond help.

Meanwhile, Richard drove throughout the night, eventually stopping to buy beer and a clothes line with which, he'd later say, he planned to hang himself. He booked into a hotel that was a hundred miles from the murder scene, lay down on the bed and fell asleep.

As he slept, his photograph was broadcast on television and someone phoned the police and gave them his current location. They surrounded his room, prepared for a shoot-out, but he surrendered quietly. He was arrested and returned to Massachusetts, where, to everyone's surprise, he pleaded not guilty to first-degree murder despite the fact that there were witnesses.

Shannon now went public about the abuse that she, her siblings and her mother had endured at her father's hands. She did so to thwart Richard Sharpe, who was demanding that he have visits from his youngest children, despite the fact that they were terrified of him.

A suicide attempt

Richard now attempted suicide by swallowing a phial of medicine whilst being treated in hospital, but the medication was merely a vaccine, which didn't put his well-being at risk. He swallowed the liquid in full view of a nurse and a prison officer, suggesting that he was posturing rather than seriously trying to take his own life. He repeatedly made threatening phone calls to his daughter Shannon's answering machine (calls which she never returned) until the prison put him into an isolation unit as a punishment.

Court

The trial, held in November 2001, contained few surprises. Karen's babysitter testified that Richard had entered the house and shot his wife. The jury also got to hear the 911 call in which Karen's understandably traumatised brother said that Richard Sharpe was the person who had fired the gun.

Richard's siblings spoke movingly about the numerous times he'd been physically assaulted and emotionally abused by their father, about how he'd turned from a good kid into an aggressive and violent teenager. Richard's sister Laura admitted that he had terrorised her throughout their childhood and she was so afraid that he would kill her during the night that she put a total of ten locks on her bedroom door.

The doctor took the stand in his own defence and described the stresses that he had endured in the weeks leading up to the murder. He'd been separated from his wife and children, had broken his pelvis and endured other health problems, was being threatened with a lawsuit at work and was jealous that Karen was dating another man. He admitted to taking five or six prescription drugs on the day of the shooting and to also drinking alcohol. As is typical with such killers, he used the passive voice when talking about the homicide, saying 'The gun went off,' rather than the more honest 'I fired the gun.'

The defence psychiatrist took the stand and described Richard's mental disorders, which ranged from borderline personality to clinical depression. He noted that his client lacked a sense of identity, was unable even to decide if he wanted to be male or female. He described the various plastic surgeries that Richard had submitted to as further proof that the man was deeply confused. The prosecution's psychiatrist concurred that the doctor probably had a personality disorder but said that he was not insane. After all, he'd gone calmly to the house and asked for Karen, had driven away after he'd shot her, got rid of the weapon and bought beer and a rope before booking himself into a hotel.

Verdict

The jury agreed with the prosecution and soon returned with a verdict of guilty of murder in the first degree. Later that week he was sentenced to a life of hard labour at the Massachusetts Correctional Institution. He broke down, screaming 'I'm sorry, I'm sorry,' but many people who knew him believed that he was crying for himself.

Further mayhem

The following spring, Richard was found guilty of offering a sizeable sum to a fellow inmate to kill the assistant district attorney, who he blamed for his life sentence. Richard was put into solitary confinement as a punishment, but tried to hang himself with his shoelaces and was transferred to Bridgewater State Mental Hospital. When he revived, he contemplated having a sex change so that he could be moved to a women's prison.

On 5th January 2009, Richard Sharpe waited until his cellmate was in another part of the prison, then he wound his bed sheet around the top bunk, looped it around his neck and hanged himself. He was found within the hour and rushed to hospital where he was formally pronounced dead.

2   Dr Robert Bierenbaum

Though a previous incidence of domestic violence and cruelty to animals put this surgeon in the frame when his wife suddenly disappeared, there is no physical proof linking him to her most-likely violent death.

The child prodigy

Robert was born on the 22nd July 1955 to Netta and Marvin Bierenbaum. Marvin was a doctor and Netta worked as his receptionist. They were very proud of Robert's high IQ and almost photographic memory which ensured that he got outstanding exam results. His sister was also brilliant and went on to become a successful psychiatrist.

In high school, Robert – who liked to be called

Bob – excelled at judo, skiing and various other sports. At seventeen he went to college and in 1977 he graduated with a degree in medicine, taking an internship at Mount Sinai Hospital in Manhattan. By then he had already earned his pilot's licence so spent many evenings and weekends flying a single-engine plane. Though supremely talented he had comparatively few social skills and many people found him blunt to the point of rudeness. He also had a penetrating stare that made many of his peers uncomfortable, though some women appreciated his intensity.

Cruelty to animals

At work, Bob found himself attracted to another young physician and they dated and got engaged, but were both working 120-hour weeks and had little time to socialise. Soon the young woman had second thoughts and broke off the engagement. Bob was enraged and let himself into her apartment when she was out in order to strangle her cat.

Marriage

By his mid-twenties Bob was chief of coronary care at Mount Sinai, a remarkable achievement for one so young. During a rare night off in 1980, he met Gail Beth Katz at a mutual friend's house. She was an attractive young woman with a history of self-harming who had taken an overdose at age 23 after a boyfriend finished with her. Bob was an academic whilst Gail had dropped out of college, but there was an undeniable sexual attraction between them and they were both Jewish, a shared religion which was important to them. At first they appeared to be in love, but Gail was soon dropping hints to friends that Bob wasn't in touch with his emotional side, that he wasn't her type. However, her mother had always wanted her to marry a Jewish doctor and Gail herself seemed enamoured of the lifestyle that she could eventually enjoy as a surgeon's wife.

They planned a lavish wedding for August 1982 but, days before, she phoned her sister in distress saying that Bob had become jealous of her kitten and had tried to drown it in the toilet bowl. The animal was terrified of him so Gail's sister took it to an animal shelter to be re-homed. Even after this incident, Gail insisted on going ahead with the wedding, saying that she could make Bob happy and that, in turn, he'd support her when she returned to university.

After marrying in a Manhattan synagogue and honeymooning in Greece (Bob would remain involved with the synagogue and would later study Hebrew), the couple settled down to married life in New Jersey. Gail enrolled on a Psychology course, telling one of her fellow students that Bob had threatened to kill her if she ever left him. Fortunately, their work and college schedules kept them apart for most of the week, but they fought loudly every Sunday when they were both at home. Gail wanted Bob to pay her attention and to socialise, but he was working so hard that he needed to be able to come home and relax. Incensed at his apparent lack of interest in her, she began to have affairs.

One night in November 1983, she was sitting on the balcony of their home and having a clandestine cigarette, having told her husband that she'd given up: she knew that he detested smoking. But he came home unexpectedly and was so angry that he strangled her into unconsciousness. The following day, she left him and, four days later, she finally reported the incident to the police.

Bob himself was so concerned about this violent incident that he went to see a therapist. The psychiatrist, in turn, was so perturbed by what she heard that she phoned Gail in Bob's presence and warned her that he was dangerous. She referred Bob to another psychiatrist who also phoned Gail to warn her. A third psychiatrist, Dr Michael Stone, talked to Bob, and the surgeon admitted partially strangling Gail's kitten and strangling his former fiancée's cat to death. He showed no remorse for these acts and the psychiatrist feared that he was in the presence of a psychopath. He met Gail and quickly realised that she showed the symptoms of Borderline Personality Disorder, and that she was a perfect victim. People with this condition fear abandonment yet also enjoy risk-taking and often indulge in self-destructive behaviour. Try as he might, Dr Stone couldn't persuade her to leave Bob.

Determined to have his advice on the record, the psychiatrist wrote a registered letter to Gail, suggesting that it was hazardous for her to live with her husband at this time and for the foreseeable future. She showed it to Bob then put it into a bank safety deposit box. Dr Michael Stone would also allege that he warned Bob's parents their son was dangerous.

A brief hiatus

The couple went into therapy with another doctor, which briefly improved their ability to communicate with each other. But, in what was surely the triumph of hope over experience, Gail brought home another two cats. Soon the shouting matches resumed and Bob told a friend that Gail made him so angry that he wanted to murder her.

Meanwhile, Gail began yet another affair.

After one fight too many, she played her hand, telling him that she wanted a divorce and that he'd have to give her half of his salary for as long as she remained single. When Bob understandably objected to this, she threatened to show Dr Michael Stone's letter to his boss and to any other hospital that he might apply to in the future for a job. His brilliant career would be over before it had fully begun.

The couple eventually went to bed on the Saturday night and, the following morning, on Sunday, 7th July 1985, they resumed fighting. Neighbours heard both of them shouting followed by a loud bang. That day, Gail didn't leave the apartment as she usually did, something that the doorman would later testify to. In fact, she was never seen again.

Later that same day, Bob left the house, drove to the airport and rented a Cessna. Soon he was flying over the Wanaque Reservoir and on to the ocean. That night, he called in at a friend's house and said that Gail had left him after a fight. When he got home he phoned his mother-in-law and said that Gail was missing but didn't report this to the police, instead cleaning the apartment until the early hours, disturbing neighbours by dragging the furniture about.

On the Monday, Bob reported his wife's

disappearance to the authorities and they visited the apartment to find that Gail hadn't taken any money or credit cards, unthinkable for a woman who loved to go shopping. She'd also left behind her cigarettes and her keys. Questioned by detectives about his movements on the day that his wife had disappeared, the surgeon lied and said that he'd been home alone until the evening. He refused on two occasions to take a lie detector test. Police were convinced that he'd murdered Gail, as were her friends and family.

Whilst still under suspicion, Bob changed his flight log so that it appeared that he hadn't flown on the 7th July but on the 8th. He also altered the records to state that he'd made several short flight checks rather than one longer flight.

He almost immediately began to date two women – who didn't know about each other's existence – and two months after Gail disappeared, he moved one of them into the marital home. She was worried that Gail might return, but Bob seemed unconcerned. Indeed, when detectives phoned him one night to say that they'd found a body that might be Gail, he asked if he could go back to sleep and identify it the following day. Bob clarified that the body wasn't Gail's. His girlfriend noticed that he was kind to Gail's two cats and that he kept her possessions, including personal items such as her diary.

No charges

Bob was upset on the occasions when one of his heart patients died, so he decided to move into plastic surgery, which had a lower mortality rate, and was soon specialising in breast reconstruction for women who had survived breast cancer. Meanwhile, police closed down the investigation into Gail's disappearance, telling her family that they were convinced the doctor had murdered her but they didn't believe they had enough evidence to win the case.

The wrong body

In May 1989, police at Staten Island fished a badly decomposed female torso from the water. The head, arms and legs had been cut off, ruling out a suicide, and the sternum had once been broken but had healed. Gail Katz had never broken this bone prior to her disappearance, yet the city identified the body as hers and her parents gave the torso a full Jewish funeral and Bob sat shiva at his parents' house for a week.

A new life

Bob Bierenbaum was now in his prime. He moved to Las Vegas, established a private plastic surgery practice and dated several beautiful women. He got himself another cat and appeared to dote on it. He told some of his girlfriends that he'd never been married but told others that Gail had probably been killed by a drug dealer or had committed suicide.

He also joined the Flying Doctors of Mercy and flew down to Mexico at least four times a year at his own expense to help children with cleft palates – the uneducated community believed that this disfigurement meant that these unfortunate youngsters were possessed by the devil, so they were ostracised and suffered terribly. Bob performed corrective surgeries on them so that they enjoyed good health and were no longer pilloried. The parents loved him and referred to him as being 'like a saviour'. Fluent in five languages, Bob could communicate well with his patients and was very good at reassuring them.

During this time, his relationships with women continued to falter and he had three broken engagements. Some felt that he was trying to rush them into marriage as, by now, he longed to be a father. He was good with other people's children and wanted to start a family before he reached his fortieth birthday.

Sleepless in Seattle

In 1993, Dr Michael Stone arrived in Seattle to address a psychiatric convention. He spoke about Gail Katz Bierenbaum's disappearance and about her dangerous husband. Even though he used false names, one of the women in the auditorium had known Gail and recognised her story. Afterwards, she apparently told Dr Stone that she had seen blood on a rug in the Bierenbaums' apartment the day after Gail's disappearance, and that the rug had disappeared shortly afterwards.

A second marriage

Oblivious that he was still being talked about, Bob continued to work and play hard. In 1993, he met a female gynaecologist, Dr Janet Chollett, and they began dating. Three months later they got engaged and, the following summer, they married in New York. The couple moved to Dakota and resumed their medical careers, Janet delivering babies whilst Bob performed breast reconstruction surgery. In November 1996 they had their first child, a girl. Bob became a stay-at-home father whilst Janet, who wanted a change from medicine, enrolled in a Law school two hundred miles away. The couple rarely saw each other for a while and Bob often slept on a fold-out bed next to his aeroplane rather than go home. When he returned to work they hired a nanny, Bob taking especial care to recruit a non-smoker. His hatred of cigarettes was well known in the community and at work, where he sometimes refused to treat patients who smoked.

The years passed and Bob remained devoted to his second wife, his daughter and his patients. But, unbeknown to him, his time as a free man was running out. The authorities were looking at his case for the third time and, in 1998, decided to exhume the body that had been buried nine years previously as Gail Katz. Using improved DNA techniques they were able to prove conclusively that the torso belonged to another young woman, a Jane Doe.

Detectives reinterviewed Dr Michael Stone, and he told them about the woman who had approached him at the seminar and said that she'd seen blood on the rug in Bob and Gail's apartment. The police then interviewed her, but she said that she'd only heard a rumour about the blood and hadn't seen it with her own eyes – but she *had* seen the red marks on Gail's neck after Bob had strangled her unconscious in 1983. She'd been so alarmed that she'd given Gail a cheque as the deposit for a new apartment, but Gail had decided to remain with Bob.

Police also interviewed some of the women that Bob had dated after Gail's disappearance and one of them told the detectives about finding the altered flight log. The following year – fourteen years after Gail's disappearance – he was indicted by a grand jury in New York.

Out on bail, Bob discussed his future with Janet. Both were convinced that he would be found not guilty, after which they might relocate to Mexico where he could continue his work with disfigured children. They also wanted to have a second child.

Dr Michael Stone testified at the hearing, recounting how alarmed he was by Bob's behaviour and saying that he'd spoken to Bob's parents about the situation at the end of November 1983. But Marvin Bierenbaum was able to prove that he was in a medical conference in Taiwan at this time, and Netta Bierenbaum swore under oath that she was ill with influenza. The prosecution had to admit that the psychiatrist's dates might be wrong.

However, they were adamant about many other details: Bob had choked Gail on a previous occasion after finding her smoking a cigarette. They'd argued yet again on the day of her disappearance, after which he'd lied to people that the doorman had seen her leave the building. He had also lied in telling detectives that he was home all day when he'd actually been out flying, and had later altered the flight log to suggest that he'd used the plane on a different date.

The defence countered that Gail had been seen at a restaurant an hour or two after her supposed death and they produced a stranger who had allegedly ogled her from a nearby table. But he described her as 'statuesque', whereas Gail was short and slim.

A doctor for the prosecution testified that Gail's body would easily have folded at the waist and could have been stuffed into a bag in her apartment. The authorities had already ascertained that a bag with a 110 lb weight inside could be thrown from a small plane, so they alleged that Bob could easily have dumped his wife's body into the Atlantic, where it might never be found.

In their summary, the defence said that Gail had had several lovers and that at least one of them had never been identified, and that she occasionally used recreational drugs and could have been killed by a drug dealer. Her body might have remained hidden or she might have been wrongly buried under another name or in an unmarked grave.

Without a body, the case against Bob Bierenbaum was purely circumstantial yet the jury took less than six hours to return with a guilty verdict. Bob paled and looked deeply shocked. When he returned for sentencing, he was given twenty years to life. He appealed but his conviction was upheld in 2002. He will become eligible for parole in August 2020.

3   Dr Geza de Kaplany

Although this murder took place back in 1962, this doctor's crime still bears retelling as one of the most shocking in recent history.

Early terror

Geza was born on 27th June 1926 in Mako, Hungary. He and his two brothers were regularly beaten by their aristocratic father and, during one particularly severe thrashing, the little boy lost an eye. The father, purportedly a wealthy baron, died when Geza was twelve years old.

Geza went to the University of Szeged to study Medicine and graduated in 1951 with honours. An arrogant young man, he went on to specialise in heart complaints, but his politics differed from that of the ruling elite and he fled to America in

1956, initially settling in Boston. He planned to practise cardiology there and was enraged to find that his qualifications weren't recognised. Instead, he had to retrain as an anaesthesiologist.

The good-looking and wealthy doctor took a post at a Californian hospital and wasted no time in seducing American women, but was dismayed when one of his conquests, a Swedish bank clerk called Ruth Krueger, became pregnant. He persuaded her to go home to have the baby, saying that he had taken out an insurance policy to support her and their child. However, when she was safely abroad, he changed the policy to name his mother as his beneficiary. He also sought spiritual back-up for his actions and was given this by a priest who told him that he shouldn't marry Ruth as she was a Protestant and he was a Catholic.

With Ruth safely out of the way, Dr de Kaplany seduced five other women, including several of the nurses at San Jose Hospital where he worked. One girl agreed to go skiing with him but was shocked to find that he'd booked them a double room at the Yosemite ski resort. When she refused to sleep with him he abandoned her, knowing that she had no transport of her own. He appeared to be completely self-centred, lacked empathy and expected women to obey his every whim.

In the summer of 1962, Geza met a former beauty queen and fellow Hungarian, Hajna Piller.

Her social-climber mother was delighted when the couple started dating and enjoyed a whirlwind romance. Hajna already had a boyfriend, a Hungarian engineer with whom she was in love, but her widowed mother insisted that she marry the aristocrat. Hajna acquiesced to keep the peace, but kept seeing her boyfriend on the side. She had met Geza in June 1962 and married him that August. She was a young and liberal 25-year-old whilst he was old-fashioned and 11 years her senior. Though Geza intended to keep sleeping with other people, he didn't expect his wife to do the same...

Revenge

Just three weeks into the marriage, a woman who was in love with the doctor told him that Hajna was still seeing her engineer boyfriend. Geza was apoplectic. The following day he went to see an attorney and said that he wanted a divorce on the grounds of his wife's adultery and that he had no intention of paying alimony, but the attorney replied that he needed proof of his wife's behaviour, not hearsay. He added that the couple could eventually divorce quietly, that no one need know the details of why they broke up.

Geza would later tell police that he went home and played the conversation over and over in his mind. He didn't want his adulterous wife to get off scot-free – he wanted her to suffer. Making his way to the hospital lab, he prepared a potion that would wreak the ultimate revenge.

An agonising death

Back at his flat, Geza pretended that he wanted to make love to Hajna, but, when she was naked, he tied her to the bed, spreadeagled on her back, before putting their stereo on full blast and donning a rubber apron to protect himself. Taking a scalpel, he made numerous cuts to her face, breasts and genitals until they were hideously disfigured. He then dabbed the acids that he had brought home from the hospital into the wounds. He warned the writhing and terrified woman not to make a sound on pain of death.

Soon, Hajna's horrific shrieks could be heard above the ear-splitting music and alarmed neighbours phoned the police, who arrived to find that large sections of her flesh had been dissolved away by the mixture of nitric, hydrochloric and sulphuric acids. One of the paramedics who tried to lift her had to be treated for acid burns. Hajna, her face unrecognisable and parts of her chest and genitalia eaten away, spent an agonising month in hospital before she died.

The doctor went on trial the following year. His lawyers wanted him to plead insanity but Geza said that he'd known exactly what he was doing, that he'd deliberately defaced his wife so that no other man would ever want her. He then insisted that photos of her injuries could not be shown in court. When he was overruled on this, he raced across the courtroom and grabbed at the offending photos, shrieking 'If I did this, I must be mad.' He subsequently claimed that he wasn't responsible due to having a split personality and the defence suggested that he'd been possessed by a demon with the somewhat exotic moniker Pierre La Roche. The prosecution was more rational and said that Geza was a jealous husband who wanted revenge.

A psychiatrist claimed that Geza de Kaplany had become a paranoid schizophrenic during his abusive childhood and, taking this into consideration, the jury opted for life imprisonment rather than the gas chamber. Immediately after the trial he was allowed to appear at a press conference, at which he said, 'I realise the awful weight of that tragedy, but I do not feel any responsibility. I was crushed by forces over which I had no control.' The remorseless doctor, a man who had always treated women with the utmost disdain, began serving his sentence in an American jail.

Then in 1975, six months before he was

officially due for parole consideration, the Taiwanese government said that they urgently needed cardiac skills such as Geza possessed, and he was flown out there as a medical missionary. Shortly afterwards, he made a public statement saying that the Californian parole board no longer had jurisdiction over him, after which he disappeared. By 1980 he was working at a hospital in Munich but, when his sadistic crime became known, he was fired.

In 2002, a Californian newspaper tracked him down to Germany, where he was living quietly with his second wife.

The septuagenarian is now a naturalised German citizen and therefore he cannot be extradited for his 1975 parole violation, much to the disgust of Hajna Piller's surviving family and friends.

4 Dr Debora Green

Did this doctor kill her children because she wanted to return to the single life or because she wanted to hurt her ex-husband? Though the evidence against her was overwhelming, she refused to admit her guilt.

A studious life

Debora was born on the 28th February 1951 to Joan and Robert Jones in Illinois. She was their second daughter. Joan kept house and Robert initially drove a van for a bakery, though he later worked his way up to management level.

Joan had been an exemplary student and was determined that her daughters would fare equally well, so she stressed the importance of scholastic accomplishment. Fortunately, the girls had high IQs. Debora excelled in everything that she attempted, from playing an instrument to learning a second language. She was also an athletic cheerleader, slender and with seemingly boundless energy.

Debora graduated valedictorian from school and did equally well at the local university, where she studied Chemistry. She wanted to be a chemical engineer but, when she heard that there were few job vacancies, switched to medical school. She was accepted at the University of Kansas but showed less talent for medicine than she had for engineering. She also had difficulty in maintaining a relationship and had a short-lived marriage to an engineer during these student years. He would later say that she put little effort into the marriage and that she could be very cold. Her first medical jobs also failed to satisfy her as she found working in A&E boring, and, when she switched to oncology, she became too upset when her patients died.

The seemingly confident schoolgirl was now metamorphosing into an increasingly anxious young woman. Whilst she'd excelled academically, she struggled to cope with the real world and her patients found her uncommunicative and aloof. She also tended to be passive-aggressive rather than saying what was really on her mind.

Second marriage

By 1977, Debora was single again, solvent and working in a Missouri hospital as a resident doctor. She dated lots of men but became increasingly fond of Mike Farrar, a medical student in his final year. He was twenty, handsome and stable whilst Debora was twenty-four but deeply insecure. He noticed that she flew into rages but put this down to the long hours she was working. Despite his doubts, they married on 26th May 1979.

The next two years were difficult as Debora suffered from frequent migraines and also needed to take sedatives in order to sleep. Later, they moved to Cincinnati as Mike got a job there. In January 1982 they had their first child, Tim. Within six weeks, Deborah hired a nanny and started a fellowship, studying haematology at the local university. Two years later they had a daughter, Lissa, and, again, she swiftly returned to work.

Unfortunately she failed her exams, which meant that she couldn't become board-certified. But Mike was doing increasingly well by now so they moved back to Missouri, where he'd been offered a medical partnership. Debora also joined a medical group but she was so distant with her patients that the group didn't make her a partner. Enraged, she went into practice on her own. She also began to abuse narcotics, which she'd initially taken for headaches and for muscular pain.

In December 1988, the couple had an unplanned third child, a girl whom they called Kelly. This time Debora didn't manage to lose the weight that she'd gained, another blow to her self-esteem. She returned to work but remained unpopular with both staff and patients. The following year she gave up medicine and took refuge in overusing prescription drugs.

A possible arson attack

On the surface, Debora now became a picture-perfect mother, taking her brood to sports practice and ballet lessons, but the other parents noticed that she often shouted at the children and complained that they were driving her mad. And she didn't do any of the boring tasks that most housewives have to do, like tidying and cleaning. Instead, she left the house in chaos whilst she sat reading books. She rarely cooked so she and the children lived off takeaway food, and the house was often littered with pizza cartons and boxes containing remnants of previous fried chicken meals. By now, Debora had gained at least three stone and always dressed in baggy, dark-coloured clothes. Her mood swings continued until eventually Mike could take no more.

In January 1994, he moved out, whereupon his wife became hysterical and abusive, but later asked if they could reconcile and move to a bigger house. Mike initially agreed, then realised that this would be a mistake. He backed off, after which the house that the family was living in mysteriously caught fire. Debora and the children had to move into Mike's apartment or they would have been homeless. Shortly afterwards, they reconciled and moved into the big house Debora had desired.

Revenge

However, the couple's marriage remained desperately unhappy and Mike found refuge in another woman's arms. Aware of his adultery, Debora turned to drink.

One teatime she gave him a sandwich she'd made earlier, an unusual occurrence. It tasted slightly bitter and, later that night, he was violently sick. He felt increasingly unwell and had vomiting, diarrhoea and a fever, spending a week in hospital whilst the doctors feared that he might die. He eventually felt better and went home to Debora, who insisted on cooking him an evening meal. Later that night, all of his symptoms returned and he was readmitted to hospital, where the doctors concluded that he must have picked up a tropical virus during a recent family holiday to Peru.

Again, he stabilised, returned home and enjoyed another of Debora's home-cooked meals, only to become desperately ill once more. His friends were convinced that his wife was poisoning him, but Mike found this impossible to believe.

He was, however, suspicious enough to search her bag, and was alarmed to find seed packets containing castor beans. The beans are highly toxic, the ricin they contain being one of the strongest poisons in nature. He also found three used syringes and phials of potassium chloride, which, in high doses, can affect the body's electrolyte balance and cause heart arrhythmia. When he asked Debora what she was going to do with the beans, she said that she planned to use them to commit suicide.

Committed

As the night wore on, Debora became drunk and hysterical, saying that she'd kill herself rather than let him move in with his new lover. The children were terrified and Mike arranged for her to be committed to a private hospital. They evaluated her as being bipolar and having suicidal urges and put her on three different sedatives. They also changed her status to that of voluntarily committed. Four days later, she signed herself out and returned home.

Mike immediately moved out. By now he had researched the symptoms of ingesting ricin and strongly suspected that Debora had been poisoning him, but he felt confident leaving the children with her as she appeared to love them and they were devoted to her.

Unfortunately, the household continued to go downhill after he left, as Debora was still drinking heavily and the children were left to fend for themselves in the dirty and cluttered villa. Sometimes Mike attempted to return the youngsters after an access visit, only to find that there was no one home. Yet Debora seemed unaware of her own mental health problems and talked to neighbours about becoming a psychiatrist.

A fatal fire

On Monday, 23rd October, Mike spent the evening with his children then returned them to Debora, who was in the process of heating up a takeaway. She ignored him and he left.

Later that night she began drunkenly phoning

and paging him, sometimes playing mind games. During one call he lost his temper and told her that she had to get her act together and take better care of the kids. She screamed back at him and sounded incensed.

Shortly after midnight, she arrived at her neighbours' place with wet hair and said, surprisingly calmly, that her house was on fire. The neighbour, who was immediately convinced that Debora had set the blaze, phoned the emergency services and alerted Mike.

Odd behaviour

When the firemen arrived, they found a woman with a little girl standing outside watching the flames, the woman serene but the child increasingly hysterical. The girl begged the firemen to save her brother and sister, who were trapped inside. The fireman asked where the children's mother was and the woman, Debora, admitted that it was her. He was nonplussed that she was so detached from events.

When Mike was told of the blaze, he was also convinced that Debora had started it to get revenge or for attention. As he drove to his former house, he expected to find all of his children waiting for him on the lawn; it didn't occur to him for a second that Debora would harm them. When he was informed that two of his children had perished in the flames, he began to cry and ask Debora what she'd done, but she merely stared expressionlessly at him.

Interview

Police interviewed Debora in the early hours of the morning and she said that she'd been woken by the fire alarm but had assumed that it had been triggered in error. She'd made four attempts to switch it off before opening her bedroom door and seeing smoke in the hall. She'd escaped by a back door then had heard her thirteen-year-old son, Tim, on the intercom, asking if he should fetch his sisters and escape by sliding down the roof on the second floor, something he'd done successfully before when he'd lost his keys. She'd told him to wait in his room for the fire brigade, a move she now admitted to the police was 'the kiss of death'.

After alerting her neighbour, Debora had returned to her own lawn and seen her ten-year-old, Lissa, standing on the garage roof. She told Lissa to jump into her arms but didn't catch her. Fortunately, Lissa survived the fall.

Officers were surprised at how easily the

former doctor referred to her two dead children in the past tense. She also spent a sizeable part of the interview denigrating her husband and swearing repeatedly. They hid their shock at her strange priorities and at the extent of her rage.

When the fire died down, investigators returned to the house and found that six-year-old Kelly and her pet Labrador had died of carbon monoxide poisoning in Kelly's bedroom. Tim had died whilst breathing in the smoke-filled air. He had also been burnt pre-mortem and, after he died, part of his body had been burnt away.

Lissa went to stay with Mike's parents whilst Debora went to a hotel and resumed drinking. Her psychiatrist found her there and had her admitted to hospital.

Meanwhile, firemen found that the blaze at her house had been deliberate, that someone had set several small fires using an accelerant. This was now a murder inquiry.

Debora continued to behave inappropriately, swearing at some of the people who attended Tim and Kelly's funeral. Her rage at Mike was much, much stronger than her love for her dead children and her remaining child.

Whodunnit

Detectives, determined to keep an open mind, began to make investigations into who might have started the fire. Mike, who was inconsolable with grief, had an alibi. Debora had claimed that she wasn't close to the flames yet the neighbours said that her hair was wet, and, the following day, she'd gone to a different hairdresser to her usual one and had singed sections cut from her fringe.

They also established that she'd gone to a garden centre many miles away to order the castor beans that they believed she'd used to poison Mike. She had arrived on two different occasions to purchase the deadly seeds.

On 22nd November 1995 they arrested her as she arrived at her daughter's ballet recital. Bail was set at three million dollars. Sent to a jail in Olathe, she was given antidepressants and tranquillisers and spent much of her time in a daze.

Mike was suffering much more than his ex-wife, as the ricin had led to bacterial poisoning and he now had to have a brain abscess drained, a potentially life-threatening operation. He also developed a heart valve infection and remained thin and weak.

The preliminary hearing

At the hearing, Debora pleaded not guilty and her defence team suggested that thirteen-year-old Tim had started the blaze as he was fascinated by fire and had set light to a couple of rubbish bins when he was eight years old and his parents were talking about divorce. They also suggested that Mike's illness had resulted from swimming in Peru and eating the local food.

The garden centre staff testified that Debora had bought the castor beans, claiming that they were for a school project. And a neighbour testified that Debora had arrived at his house to report the fire with wet hair and that she seemed distant from events.

Debora remained detached in court until they were about to show photographs of her dead children, whereupon the defence shepherded her from the court. Jurors had to look at slides of Tim's feet, which had burnt away from the rest of his body. It was an unnecessary death as he could have escaped via the roof if his mother hadn't told him to go back inside.

Confession

As the trial neared, Debora admitted to her attorneys that she'd started the fire, though she said she had been so drunk she hadn't known what she was doing. Her psychiatrist talked to her and Debora claimed that Tim had poisoned his dad.

Debora decided to plead no contest to the arson charges, which meant that there was no trial and she no longer faced the death penalty. On 30th May 1996, she was sentenced for forty years in jail and was transferred to the Topeka Correctional Institute in Kansas to serve her sentence. Now, as before, she could spend most of her days reading books.

Later, Debora recanted her confession and appealed her sentence, only to change her mind again and drop the appeal. She will be in her mid-eighties before she is released.

5   Dr Dirk Greineder

Though this allergist was found guilty of murdering his wife of thirty-two years, he had comparatively little motive.

A scholastic childhood

Dirk was born on the 19th October 1940 in Berlin, Germany, the second son of Renee Chaoun and Kurt Greineder. When he was five, the family moved to Beirut in Lebanon, where he remained until he was eighteen. By then, he could speak four languages: German, French, English and Arabic.

Moving to America, Dirk attended Yale and majored in Biochemistry before studying for a masters degree in Medicine and Pharmacology at a Cleveland university, meeting his future wife, Mabel (always known as May) Chegwin there. She was studying for an advanced degree in Nursing and went on to become an assistant professor at a local nursing school.

On 7th July 1967, the couple married and, in 1970, Dirk completed his studies. The following year, May gave birth to their first child, a daughter, and the couple doted on her. They went on to have two other children. In 1972, Dirk became a research fellow at Boston's Robert B Brigham Hospital and later became a respected allergist.

A loving family

May stayed at home until their three children were adults. They loved to swim competitively and she and Dirk took them to all of their swim meets. They appeared to be happy although Dirk could be somewhat controlling and May had to run all of her decisions past him.

The children worried about how their mother would cope when they left the nest, but May returned to work, as a triage nurse, in 1993. She remained in nursing for the next five years and then left the profession to care for her dying mother. Her sister paid May's transport costs as Dirk wanted her to keep to a tight budget. He didn't visit his mother-in-law in the months leading up to her death. In September 1999, May enrolled at college to study for another nursing degree. By then she had lost weight, had a facelift (also paid for by her sister) and was making the most of her middle years.

A shocking murder

On 31st October 1999, Dirk and May enjoyed their usual Sunday morning routine, whereby he made breakfast and they ate together, did a little academic work and took care of various chores.

It was still early in the morning when they dressed and took one of their dogs to Morses Pond, beloved by many of the locals in Wellesley, Massachusetts. Some time later, Dirk called the police from his car phone to say that his wife had been attacked and was possibly dead.

He said that May had slipped on the path and hurt her back so she'd insisted that he walk their Alsatian alone, explaining that she'd rest and catch up with him. But the dog had been anxious so he'd returned after ten minutes to find her lying motionless at the foot of an embankment. He'd felt for her pulse and found a large gash in her neck. The police arrived and he told them the same story, then asked, 'Are you going to arrest me?' He also volunteered the rather unusual information that his wife had given him a back rub that morning so his skin would be under her fingernails.

Noticing that May's trousers had been pulled down to expose her stomach, the police wondered if she'd been raped. They knew that they'd have to rule out marital sex so asked Dirk if he had recently been intimate with his wife, but he said that they had not been sexually active for the last few years.

Dirk had told them that he'd checked his wife's carotid artery yet there was no blood on his hands, but they could see that there were spots of what looked like blood on his jacket, trainers and even his spectacles, though they didn't test the latter as Dirk insisted that he needed them to drive home. They settled for photographing his glasses and this photograph would later be shown in court.

Detectives searched the section of the woods where he had walked and found a hammer, knife and glove, all of which were bloodstained, hidden in a storm drain. The doctor was becoming a suspect and he was read his Miranda rights.

A police photographer found scratches on his neck and chest and some fingertip-sized bruises on one of his arms. They theorised that he had planned to kill May with one blow from the hammer but that she had remained conscious and had screamed – another dog walker in the area had heard a woman screaming. They alleged that he had hit her again and that she'd grabbed hold of him, leaving blood on his jacket. They claimed that she had then fallen to the ground and he had cut her throat and stabbed her ten times.

Searching his house and garage, they found that he had prescribed himself Viagra and had bought a box of condoms. Investigating his computer, they found that he had been emailing swingers' chat rooms and had paid to join Internet porn sites. He had booked hotel rooms in the name of his college room-mate, Thomas Young, and had met prostitutes there. On their own, these events weren't particularly damning – after all, some men crave sexual variety, especially when they fear they are ageing and their virility is declining. But a lust-filled man might want his wife out of the way...

Trial

On 29th February 2000, police arrested the doctor and, the following day, a grand jury indicted him. He pleaded not guilty. By now, tests had ascertained that it was May's blood on the hammer, knife and glove found in the storm drain, whilst Dirk's DNA was found on the handle of the knife and on the glove. Imprisoned, he lost over two stone and aged visibly.

In July, a prostitute told the grand jury that she'd met Dirk Greineder (who was using his alias of Thomas Young) in a hotel room and had had sex with him. He'd been visibly nervous and had given her chocolates, flowers and champagne.

The trial began on 21st May 2001 in Norfolk, Massachusetts. The jury was taken to Morses Pond and also shown photographs of the scene of the crime. The prosecution said that Dirk had killed his wife because he wanted to be free to meet up on a regular basis with swingers and prostitutes; that May could have found out about his activities and asked for a divorce and a financial settlement. They alleged that he had chosen a public place because a man and a woman had been murdered in similar locations and the killer or killers had never been found. Dirk had saved both murder reports on his computer, indicating that he was aware of this local killer-on-the-loose.

The jury also heard that a receipt for a hammer had been found in the Greineder's garage, bought the month before May was murdered with such a tool.

Dirk had contacted an escort girl in June, four months before his wife's death, and arranged then cancelled a rendezvous. He was clearly conflicted. He had also sent a naked photograph of himself to a couple but they had never finalised a time to meet up.

The defence also scored a point: the DNA of three different unknown people had been found on one of the gloves May had been wearing when she was slaughtered. And, though the police said that blood hadn't been found on Dirk's hands, he could have wiped them on his jacket. They had failed to do an orthotoluidine test.

Dirk Greineder took the stand and said that his sexual dalliances had been very much secondary to his love for his wife, that he'd met a prostitute for the first time in February 1998 and gone on to have sex with another eight women, some of whom were escort girls and others swingers. He had also joined a dating site looking for casual sex.

May had found his Viagra and had been upset but he'd reassured her that, as a doctor, he was merely experimenting with the drug. He said that she probably knew that he was having extra-marital sex but that she hadn't questioned him about this.

He painted a picture of himself as a loving husband who also wanted extra-marital sexual excitement. For example, the day before the murder he'd called a prostitute but, that night, he'd helped May write an essay for her college course. They were intellectual equals, whereas most of the women that he met for sex were uneducated and comparatively inarticulate. The day after his wife's death he had phoned an escort girl and cancelled a forthcoming liaison, telling her that this was not a good time for him.

The prosecution made a great deal of these liaisons, pointing out that he'd asked one prostitute if he could shower with her and if he could perform oral sex on her. She'd refused both offers but agreed to straight sex. He'd spent hours surfing the net for porn sites and had watched a porn movie in his hotel one night after attending a medical conference, but this was hardly a motive for murdering the love of his life.

The couple's children took the stand in their father's defence and it was clear that they'd loved their parents very much. His son Colin said that he'd become aware of his father's interest in porn whilst using his computer. He'd asked his mother if they were happy and she'd hinted that his father was finding sex elsewhere.

In summary, Dirk Greineder's defence team pointed to the lack of motive and also asked why a trained pharmacologist, with access to numerous poisons, would choose to batter his wife to death in a public location. If he had planned to murder her, why hadn't he erased the history of his computer to hide the fact that he'd been accessing porn sites and contacting swingers' clubs?

At the end of the five-week trial, the jury began their deliberations, drawing up a timeline of the day of the murder. Dirk – and Dirk alone – had been seen near the storm drain where the murder weapons were found. He said he'd seen a shadow but no one else had noticed this. They were also convinced by the blood spatter evidence; if the doctor hadn't been standing near his wife when she was being beaten he wouldn't have had so many drops of blood on his clothes and spectacles. After deliberating for thirty-one hours, they reached a guilty verdict and the allergist was sentenced to life imprisonment without the possibility of parole.

In May 2006, Dirk's appeal – based on the fact that the jury shouldn't have been told about his secret obsession with prostitutes – was denied. He also lost his bid for a second trial.

6 Dr Jonathan Nyce

When his mail-order bride was unfaithful to him, this biologist became fatally violent.

A Filipino bride

Though he was a highly regarded molecular biologist in New Jersey, Dr Jonathan Nyce failed at relationship after relationship with women. He was too possessive and, at age forty, was still single and often alone. Determined to marry and have children, he began a pen pal relationship with a beautiful nineteen-year-old Filipino girl, Michelle, from an impoverished family, telling her that he was only thirty-one.

The wealthy doctor flew out to the Philippines in 1990 to meet her and fell in love, and it seemed that the feeling was mutual. They married shortly afterwards and he brought her back to his mansion on millionaires' row. The lovely young girl who was used to sharing a makeshift house with six brothers and sisters now had a very palatial home.

Jonathan had his pride so he told his colleagues that Michelle was the assistant of a medical professor, that he'd met her in Hawaii at a medical conference. With the jewellery and expensive outfits that he'd bought her, she looked every inch the professional.

Over the next few years, the couple had three children and Nyce's career – he ran his own business specialising in asthma treatment – rose to even greater heights. He spent much of this money on others, sending cash gifts to his wife's parents and building a children's playground in their village in the Philippines.

When the couple's own children started nursery school, Michelle became bored and restless. Jonathan was working long hours and she wanted to go back to work. The doctor, however, liked to be able to keep checks on her and would frequently phone her mobile and ask to speak to her companions, just to make sure that she'd told the truth about the friends that she was with that day. He didn't want her to join the gym or a running group as she'd be in contact with other men there. He also disapproved of the figure-hugging dresses she wore, but she had a fantastic figure and wanted to look good.

Adultery

In 2002, the doctor hired a gardening firm to landscape his estate and Miguel DeJesus arrived to carry out the work. He and Michelle began an affair and they frequently met in hotel rooms for sex.

The Nyces' circumstances changed drastically the following year when the doctor's business began to fail and he had to sell his controlling shares to pay off his increasing debts. He continued to struggle financially and the company went into receivership.

Unemployed, he began to spend every day at home, making it difficult for Michelle to sneak out to see her lover. She got a job as a cosmetics rep in an upmarket department store but this caused further problems as Jonathan wanted her to be at home for their offspring during the long summer holiday. He wrote a book of poetry for children but failed to find a publisher and became increasingly depressed. He was also aware that Michelle resented him being around, as she told him that it was 'her house' during the day.

Also that summer, Michelle found that her lover was seeing two other women. When he asked her to lend him money, she took umbrage and wanted to end the relationship. She told her husband about the affair and he angrily phoned Miguel DeJesus and warned him, in no uncertain terms, to stay away. Undaunted, DeJesus said that he'd taped some of his sex sessions with Michelle and that, if Jonathan didn't pay him $500,000, he'd release them to the couple's family and friends.

The doctor reported this blackmail threat to the police and a judge granted a temporary restraining order, keeping DeJesus away from the Nyces' estate until the alleged crime could be fully investigated.

By the New Year, Michelle had foolishly returned to her lover. She again began to meet him in hotel rooms, telling her husband that she was with friends. Jonathan was suspicious as she would return home glowing with happiness and looking freshly showered...

A violent death

A showdown was inevitable and it happened in the early hours of 17th January 2004, a particularly stormy night. Michelle had spent so long with her lover that it was the early hours of the morning before she crept back to the marital home, expecting her husband to be fast asleep. But Jonathan confronted her in the garage, they quarrelled and he beat her to the ground. He'd later say that she went for him with a stiletto (but such a shoe was never found), that he had pushed her out of the way and she had hit her head against the concrete floor, dying instantly.

But Jonathan's subsequent actions were not those of a man who hadn't intended to take a life. He lifted his wife's body into her car, drove to a creek that was less than a mile away and pushed the vehicle down an embankment into the swirling water. He hoped that it would look as if she'd careered off the road during the night's storm.

Detectives were immediately suspicious as Jonathan kept close tabs on his wife yet hadn't phoned around to find out where she was or reported her to the police as a missing person. He also refused to let Michelle's best friend near the garage and kept talking about her affair rather than mourning her death. Investigators found blood in the garage, a bloody trail leading to the bathroom and bloodstained towels hidden in the chimney. There was also proof that someone had used chemicals to clean up further pools of blood.

Michelle's body was badly battered but her injuries hadn't been caused by crashing her car.

Indeed, the vehicle had slid so gently into the water that it was barely scratched and the windscreen was still intact.

Charged with first-degree murder, Jonathan described the death as a stupid accident. He wept and pointed out that he had no criminal record or previous history of violence.

At his trial in Trenton, New Jersey, in June 2005, the prosecutor noted that Jonathan had at first tried to blame the death on his wife's blackmailing lover. When that failed, he'd said that Michelle, looking drugged, had lunged at him with a stiletto and that she'd died whilst he was defending himself, adding that he'd thrown the shoe out of the window as he drove her body to the creek, but the shoe was never found.

The defence said that Michelle could have died in her car and said that, if Dr Nyce had wanted to murder his wife, he could have used his medical knowledge to kill her in a way that would have gone undetected. He had adored her and been deeply hurt by her affair.

The jury found him guilty of passion/ provocation manslaughter and he was sentenced to five to ten years with a further eighteen months for tampering with the evidence.

7 Dr John Cavaness

Though outwardly a respected GP, Cavaness murdered throughout the 1970s and early '80s, sometimes by accident whilst drink-driving, at other times deliberately for financial gain.

Attacked on all sides

John, who was always known by his middle name of Dale, was born on 15th October 1925 and endured an unhappy childhood in southern Illinois. His Calvinist mother believed in predestination, that a deity had chosen, before birth, which people would go to heaven and which to hell. Being wealthy was apparently a sign that you might have been chosen, so she dressed Dale in expensive – and somewhat effeminate – clothing. As a result, he got beaten up repeatedly at school.

One day his father saw him being chased by a gang of pupils and told Dale that, if he didn't fight back, he'd beat him again when he got home. Faced with violence from all sides, Dale began to retaliate and would eventually become such a remorseless streetfighter that he despised anyone weaker, anyone who showed fear or pain.

Against his parents' wishes, Dale married his high school sweetheart but the marriage failed when she fell in love with one of his friends; he was inconsolable. He escaped his home town to study Medicine in St Louis and fell in love with a beautiful nurse called Marian, who was religious like his parents but much more fun-loving and fashionable.

Marian, who had lost her own mother to cancer when she was just thirteen, was devoted to Dale and, after he graduated, she gave up her work and friends to return to his impoverished rural home town, where women were expected to be content with doing the housework. Dale set up a thriving medical practice there and seemed desperate to show his critical mother, whom he hated, that he was a success.

He became violent towards Marian on their first wedding anniversary in 1953 when they were on their third bottle of champagne and she said lightly that she hoped they wouldn't have to live in Illinois for ever. Dale hit her so hard in the face that he knocked her to the floor. Unfortunately she forgave him for this assault, and the others which followed, and bore him four sons between 1954 and 1966.

A cruel father

Dale Cavaness proved to be as brutal a father as he was a husband and regularly beat his four children – Mark, Kevin, Patrick and Sean – with a paddle for supposed infractions. He beat them again if they cried, because he'd been raised to hate any sign of weakness. He was also emotionally abusive, telling them that they were stupid and worthless, that he wished they'd never been born. His assaults on Marian also increased, as invariably happens with domestic violence, and he blackened her eyes, fractured her arm and broke her thumb.

Dale showed other signs of sociopathy, drinking and driving on a regular basis and speeding so recklessly that, on several occasions, he ended up in a ditch and had to buy a new car. He bought farm property and cattle for investment purposes but shot his prize bull dead when it proved difficult to handle. He was equally merciless whilst out shooting, indifferent to the suffering of the birds he wounded but didn't kill outright.

Dale borrowed heavily to invest in dubious get-rich-quick schemes and was visibly enraged when they failed to perform well or collapsed completely. He also alienated most of the nurses that he employed, as he would seduce them with honeyed words, take them to bed, then quickly lose interest, treating them thereafter as if they were the lowest form of animal life. But the locals loved him as he'd grown up in the same impoverished area and didn't hassle his poorest patients when they couldn't pay their bills. He possibly identified with their plight, as he'd been so broke during medical school that he'd frequently had to sell his own blood to survive.

Constantly in need of his next adrenalin charge, Dale Cavaness became more and more addicted to violence and to whisky. He kept bottles of spirits in his office, car and home and would turn up at his medical practice with a hangover, then take amphetamines to get him through the day. Increasingly desperate for cash to fund his habit and his failing investments, he illegally sold liquid morphine to a convicted felon and threatened to kill a witness if he told anyone.

Two vehicular homicides

On 8th April 1971, Dale was driving his truck whilst intoxicated when he crashed into a Plymouth car, virtually demolishing it. Donald McLaskey, aged twenty-nine, was thrown from the vehicle and died instantly whilst his young wife, Dorothy, was badly injured and spent several days in a coma. Their ten-month-old baby, Deidrea, died after being impaled on the outside mirror of the car.

Dr Cavaness was arrested at the scene and was so drunk that he couldn't sign his name. Two and a half hours later, a fellow doctor told him that a father and baby were dead and that the mother was fighting for her life, but Dale's only response was a slurred 'Everybody's got to die sometime.' Incredibly, he was let off with a fine as the authorities didn't want to impose a prison sentence – something that would result in the doctor losing his licence to practise medicine.

But Dale's reckless behaviour was the last straw for the long-suffering Marian and, in August 1971, she left him and took all four of their sons with her, relocating to St Louis. Unfortunately, their oldest son, Mark, now a young adult, missed his former friends and returned to Illinois to work on one of his dad's farms, living in a trailer nearby.

Mark's murder

At Easter 1977, Mark asked his mother and brothers to come to southern Illinois to celebrate the holiday with him. But, when they arrived at

Dale's house as arranged, Mark wasn't there. Marian asked her ex-husband what could have happened and Dale replied that he had a funny feeling that his son was dead. Telling him not to be ridiculous, several family members explored the area close to Mark's trailer and discovered him lying in the grass. He had been shot through the heart with one of Dale's shotguns, after which his corpse had been partially eaten by animals.

Questioned by police, Dale said that he assumed the 22-year-old had committed suicide as his life showed little promise. He seemed indifferent to his oldest son's death. Police discovered that he'd taken out an insurance policy on Mark only two months before, a policy that would now net him $40,000 – money he badly needed to pay his debts.

Detectives were convinced that he'd killed his firstborn for the insurance money, but they couldn't prove it, so Dale Cavaness was given the cash and promptly repaid his loans.

Sean's murder

For the next seven years, Dale continued to cause mayhem, starting fights, getting arrested and smashing up his cell. Whenever he had contact with his surviving sons, he was verbally and sometimes physically abusive. He was also so insulting during his phone calls to Marian that she suffered from ongoing stress.

Sean, his fourth child, was the most strongly affected by this maltreatment and was desperate to win his father's love. He took to drink for a couple of years, but did well in an Alcoholics Anonymous centre, and his mood lifted further when he got a supportive girlfriend.

Dale seemed pleased with his son's progress and suggested he insure him – and his two other remaining brothers, Kevin and Patrick – for $100,000 each. He said that the policies would mature in a few years and provide funds for their future. He also took out another two policies on Sean with different companies, which were together worth another $40,000. Sean Cavaness was now worth much more dead than alive...

On 12th December 1984, Dale drove for several hours until he reached Sean's house in St Louis, only to find that his youngest son was out. Dale had told no one of his plan to visit. He drove slowly around the area and looked so suspicious that a housewife peeking out of the window wrote down his car registration number, thinking that he had burglary on his mind. She watched her neighbour, Sean, come into view, whereupon the man parked, left his vehicle and hugged the youth. The woman now recognised the driver as

Sean's father, Dr Dale Cavaness, whom she'd met with Sean once before.

Unaware that he had been observed, Dale took Sean to a local bar and plied him with drink, despite knowing that Sean was on an anti-alcohol programme. When the 22-year-old was so drunk that he could hardly stand, he drove him to a lonely farm road next to a sealed-off contaminated area and made an excuse for them to leave the car. Dale, who had deliberately remained sober, held his gun an inch away from the back of Sean's head and fired, the bullet exiting under the young man's left eye. He fell to the ground and Dale shot him again, removed all forms of identification from the corpse then quickly drove home and attended a local pre-Christmas party. No one, including his live-in girlfriend, noticed anything different about him.

Sean's body was found the following day by a sheep farmer, one of the few people in weeks who had stopped by the dioxin-contaminated site. The youth was identified through his fingerprints; he had once been stopped by the police and had his prints taken for a misdemeanour, namely failing to yield to an emergency vehicle. Dale Cavaness was doubtlessly shocked as he hadn't expected the body to be found for some time, leading to uncertainty about the time of death.

Dale told the police that he hadn't seen Sean for

weeks – but when informed that a neighbour of Sean's had identified him, he changed his story. He said that they'd gone for a drive together and that they'd been driving past the contaminated site when Sean said that he needed to get out and urinate. He added that Sean had taken him by surprise by suddenly turning Dale's gun on himself and committing suicide. He knew that Marian would be upset if she thought that another of her sons had taken his own life so he, Dale, had fired a second shot to make it look like a homicide, then had wiped Sean's fingerprints from the .357 Magnum and driven swiftly home.

Detectives listened in growing disbelief to the doctor's far-fetched tale. At one stage he used the name of Mark instead of Sean, and they realised that he saw his sons as indistinguishable from each other, that they were as disposable to him as the game birds that he loved to kill.

Charged with Sean's murder, he began a campaign to clear his name. Most of his impoverished patients backed him up, and dozens of them wrote letters to the local press saying that the doctor was being framed by big city detectives. In turn, detectives searched his office and found a two-pound sledgehammer, a ten-inch butcher's knife and a cord knotted with a hangman's noose.

The ones that got away

Gradually, the authorities realised that Dale had probably intended to continue his killing spree. His second son, Kevin, told police that he'd woken up one day to find the holiday caravan that his father had provided for him was full of gas, as all four of the gas rings on the cooker had mysteriously been turned on during the night. He knew that his father had a substantial life insurance policy out on him...

However, determined to support their GP, the locals turned up in droves to champion Dale Cavaness at his trial, and, when they noticed that he'd lost a lot of weight, they blamed this on the stress of being framed for murder. In reality, fathers (and mothers) who kill are often heavy drinkers who lose weight in jail because they no longer have access to calorific alcohol.

The prosecution built an irrefutable case against the sociopathic doctor who cared little for human life. His family described the numerous beatings they'd suffered at his hands, and a ballistics expert noted that Sean's wounds weren't consistent with suicide. However, by mistake, the jury were given the doctor's polygraph results, despite the fact that these were inadmissible in Missouri. This legal error resulted in a mistrial, much to Dale's delight.

The second trial was held in St Louis in mid-November 1985. The jury heard about Dale Cavaness's lethal drinking and driving, about the substantial debts he'd incurred over the years through his poor investments, many of which were still outstanding. His creditors were clamouring to be paid.

In court, he showed no emotion as he looked at his son Sean's autopsy photographs. He told them that Sean had been masochistic, that he enjoyed being abused by Dale and liked having something to complain about to his mother. He was equally dismissive of his ex-wife and remaining sons.

The jury were out for less than three hours before returning with a verdict of guilty. At the penalty phase, they recommended that the sixty-year-old be put to death.

A still-remorseless Dale Cavaness was transferred to the state penitentiary at Jefferson City to await his date with the gas chamber. On Death Row, he spent his time composing his autobiography, writing to his fan club and reading medical magazines, but psychologists would later speculate that he hated the prospect of being killed by the state as this would rob him of the control he had fought for all his life. Instead, he plotted to die on a day of his choosing and by his own hand.

On 17th November 1986, he waited until the

other inmates were asleep then looped an electrical extension cord around his neck and tied it around the bars of the door. By raising his feet off the ground, he was able to slowly strangle himself to death. It was a painful demise that required courage and staying power, but Dale Cavaness had been raised to withstand pain.

It is also believed that he left a suicide note proclaiming his innocence in an attempt to cause as much mayhem and confusion as possible, and most likely hoped that his family would feel guilty for testifying against him.

8   Sinedu Tadesse

The enormous pressure brought about by moving from her native Ethiopia to America caused this already damaged medical student to have a breakdown, with fatal consequences for her room-mate.

Feeling alienated

Sinedu was born in 1974 to Atsede and Tadesse Zelleke in Addis Ababa, Ethiopia. Her mother was a nurse in a government hospital and her father was a headmaster. She would later describe them as shy and lonely, and say that they acted as if emotions didn't exist.

Sinedu had two sisters and two brothers but found it difficult to bond with others, even her relatives. Sensitive but outwardly composed, she took refuge in academic work at her Catholic school. She sat alone on school trips and felt lonely and unpopular but didn't know how to connect.

When she was seven, her father was sent to prison for two years for ostensibly having rebel sympathies, whereupon the family became increasingly impoverished and her mother became depressed and angry. Later, Sinedu would describe these years as 'empty' and 'hellish'. As there was a great deal of tribal violence in Ethiopia, she lived in a culture of mistrust and hate.

As a teenager, Sinedu was averagely attractive but very plainly dressed, refusing to wear shorts during gym class as she thought that this was immodest. Many Ethiopian women walk with their eyes downcast and don't draw attention to themselves but Sinedu took this to extremes and found it almost impossible to speak in company.

She won a scholarship to the best secondary school in her region but was amongst wealthy children and this increased her sense of isolation. Many of them were Westernised but Sinedu remained a traditionalist, who her guidance teacher described as 'incapable of individual expression'. The shy young student kept hoping that, if she could win a place at Harvard and become a doctor, she would find some self-confidence.

Sinedu achieved her goal (an impressive feat as only 14% of Harvard applications are accepted), moved to the States and at first lived with her cousins, who had emigrated to America many years previously. However, she wasn't close to them and preferred to confide in her diary. She also recorded her problems onto a cassette recorder, played it back and tried to think of solutions. She wished that she had a friend that she could go out to lunch with or with whom she could share a shopping trip. Psychiatrists would later speculate that she was suffering from Avoidant Personality Disorder, which may have cumulated in a violent manic episode.

In her freshman year, Sinedu moved into one of Harvard's student houses and shared a room with a girl called Anna. They weren't close but Sinedu assumed that the arrangement would continue the following year. Instead, Anna told her that she was moving in with someone else, leaving Sinedu feeling rejected and alone. Another pre-med student of the same age, a girl called Trang Phuong Ho who was in one of her science classes, offered to room with her instead.

The new room-mate

Trang was a happy, well-adjusted pre-med student from Vietnam who had lots of friends and was enjoying her studies. She was kind to Sinedu, as she was to everyone, and sometimes they ate together at an Ethiopian restaurant, but

93

Sinedu saw it as a special friendship, writing in her diary that she would make Trang 'the queen of her life'. She was consequently hurt and enraged when her room-mate continued to socialise with other students, helped to run the Harvard Vietnamese Students' Association and spent time with family members. Sinedu spent hours crying in their room when Trang was out and sometimes deliberately failed to pass on Trang's phone messages.

Sinedu had planned to return to Ethiopia after qualifying as a doctor – she specifically wanted to be a dermatologist, perhaps because her Ethiopian home was close to a leper colony and she wanted to help local people – but now she struggled with some of her studies and was no longer top of the class as she had been at home. She found it difficult to write essays that required a personal opinion as she had spent most of her school days learning by rote. She often borrowed Trang's notes from science class but refused to lend her own.

During their second year of rooming together, Sinedu spiralled into a clinical depression and became increasingly untidy. She left food to spoil in their room and this attracted an insect infestation, but when Trang confronted her about the situation Sinedu became both defensive and aggressive. She plotted to kill some of Trang's friends and anyone else who she thought was deliberately ignoring her.

The twenty-year-old prayed every morning but her prayers, to have friends, went unanswered and she wrote in her notebook that she was unable to make people respond to her. She was almost autistic in her inability to understand human relationships and her angst grew and grew.

Desperate to reach out, she wrote a letter saying that she lived in her own shell, afraid to express her opinions. She wrote, 'All my life I have been plagued with social problems... When I am with one person I shake with nervousness fearing that we will run out of things to say.' She photocopied this letter and sent it to random names she picked out of the phone book. One woman responded but Sinedu sent her a rambling cassette tape in which she spoke only of her numerous troubles. Alarmed at this level of self-obsession, her potential new friend didn't respond.

In the spring of their junior year, Trang told Sinedu that she didn't want to room with her again in the new academic year, that she'd chosen others to share accommodation with. Sinedu was devastated and begged the twenty-year-old to reconsider, saying that she was already distraught because Trang spent some of her time with other friends. Trang replied that she respected Sinedu but that their living requirements were different.

The Ethiopian student's resources were now at an all time low – she had no one to live with for the coming academic year so would be allocated a room-mate at random, probably someone who was equally unpopular. She was failing her science classes and could see that her future as a dermatologist was slipping away.

However, Sinedu cheered up briefly when she decided to commit suicide and, now that the pressure to interact had been taken away, she started to wear make-up and trendy clothes. More chillingly, she also bought two large knives and a length of nylon rope. She skipped her neurobiology and chemistry exams, acts that were completely out of character as she normally arrived first for all of her exams. As her mental health declined further, she sent a photograph of herself to the student newspaper with an anonymous note that said there would soon be exciting gossip concerning the girl in the photograph...

The murder

On what was to be the last night of her life, Trang watched a video with a female friend called Thao and at 2 a.m. they returned to Trang's room, where the friend stayed over, sleeping head to toe. Sinedu was lying on her bed with the light on but didn't acknowledge them.

At breakfast time on 28th May 1995, Thao awoke to find Sinedu stabbing Trang with a huge knife. Trang was trying to defend herself with her hands, so shocked that she was beyond speech. Thao tried to grab the blade but only succeeded in cutting her palm. During the struggle, Sinedu also stabbed Thao in the foot. Bleeding heavily, she ran to get help but, to her horror, the heavy door shut and self-locked behind her. She alerted other students who summoned the emergency services. They arrived to find that Trang had been stabbed repeatedly in the neck, chest and arms. Medics found a total of forty-five stab wounds to her slender body: in other words, overkill. Strangely, Trang's body was found lying next to Sinedu's bed and Thao was convinced that the murderer had carried her there.

Entering the shower room, police found that Sinedu had hanged herself from a rope secured to a heavy curtain rod. She had premeditated her suicide, cutting the rope to length on her bedside cabinet and leaving the excess coiled there.

A bitter irony

Sinedu Tadesse was much more popular in death than she was in life, with several thousand people attending her funeral. Thao, who was stabbed whilst trying to save her friend Trang, subsequently had two operations to repair the deep wounds to her hand.

9 Virginia McGinnis

Four people died in mysterious circumstances whilst in the presence of this home care nurse, including her mother, daughter and second husband, but it was only when she killed a non-relative that her life of crime was brought to an end.

Early hell

Virginia was born in 1937 to Mary and Christie Hoffman. He had been drummed out of the police force for drunkenness so the couple now ran a small farm in Ithica. They also had a son, Tom.

The family lived in squalor and Virginia was so dirty and unkempt that she was ostracised by the local children. She often came to school without a packed lunch and sometimes stole food from the other pupils. She also ate food intended for the pigs.

At home, she and her brother were frequently beaten and she was sexually assaulted by a male relative. Virginia was known to torture small animals and was later suspected of poisoning her mother's pet dogs; she was becoming a psychopath.

At seventeen, she married a local boy, Dick Coates, and they had a son but she was soon having sex with other men and the marriage descended into mutual violence, yet they went on to create a second son together. The relationship remained volatile and Dick woke up one night to find the house in flames. He and the children were lucky to get out alive.

Virginia was determined to put her appalling childhood behind her and began to dress as a lady and tell strangers that she'd had a wealthy upbringing. She passed bad cheques in clothing shops and was arrested at the age of twenty-two. She was put on probation but this did nothing to quell her need for excitement and her peers were suspicious the following year when her marital home again went up in flames. Dick stayed in the marriage until their oldest child was eleven, then ordered his wife to leave. She did so and, much to everyone's surprise, went back to her father. Dick continued to pay maintenance for his sons. Two years after the split, Virginia was living in California and gave birth to a girl, Cynthia, by another man.

Cynthia's death

In June 1972, Virginia married Bud Rearden, who was in the navy. By now she was working as a homecare nurse, tending an elderly woman. Her mother was also working as a nurse at a veterans' hospital. Virginia told some of her neighbours that she was a registered nurse but this would later prove to be a lie; her nursing skills were basic and she was more interested in her patients' valuables than in maximising their health.

On 6th December 1972, Virginia contacted the authorities to say that she'd found her three-year-old daughter, Cynthia, dead in the barn, hanging from some gardening twine. Though detectives were suspicious, the official line was that it was a tragic accident.

Bud's death

Bud was later diagnosed with cancer and Virginia nursed him at home; she regularly gave him his painkilling injections. She often struck his teenage sons from a former marriage, but on 7th September 1974 was nice to them and gave them money to go out for the day, though she warned them that their father could die at any time.

They arrived home late that night to find

Bud dead – and, by the time that the authorities were contacted, Virginia's mother had washed and cleaned the body rather than waiting for the doctor to attend. Bud's death was attributed to the cancer that had been stealing his energy. Shortly after his burial, Virginia's house burnt down; by now, almost every house that she had ever lived in had gone up in flames. Psychologists would later speculate that these arson attacks fed her need for excitement, a need that is common in those with sociopathic tendencies.

Another marriage

In 1983, Virginia met a small-time crook called Billy Joe McGinnis – known as BJ. He'd spent most of his life as a hustler on the gay scene but had married five times hoping to live off the latest woman in his life. In time, they had all seen through him and thrown him out. Virginia excelled at putting on airs and graces, and wore good jewellery, so he wrongly deduced that she had cash.

The couple married on 14th April 1984, after which Virginia gave up work and Billy found that her only income was a small disability cheque. Virginia was equally dismayed to find that BJ was broke and without prospects, just a good-looking drifter. They'd hoped to scam each other but now they'd have to dupe someone else.

Another suspicious death

The McGinnis tribe remained unusually accident-prone, telling their insurance company in 1985 that Virginia's mother's home had burnt to the ground. The company reimbursed her. Virginia's mother, Mary, bought a new home for herself and let Virginia live there. The latter told the children that Mary could die at any time. They were surprised as, though she was a diabetic, she was responding well to insulin; indeed, Virginia often administered the stabilising shots. Within hours of Virginia warning that Mary might die, she did so. Virginia had her cremated the day after and soon collected the insurance policy.

In March 1986 a windstorm allegedly damaged Virginia's home and the company again paid out, but the family's misfortunes continued in October of that year when they were burgled and lost thousands of dollars' worth of property. Two days later, their house was flooded and again they received large sums of compensation from their insurance company.

Deana's murder

Virginia now befriended a younger woman, twenty-year-old Deana Hubbard Wild, who had moved to the area after her marriage broke up. Deana had dated Virginia's son James a couple of times whilst he was out on parole – he'd murdered a drug dealer – but he violated the terms of his release and was soon returned to jail. Deana was a friendly, learning-disabled girl in a new area, so she was very glad of the McGinnis's company. She moved in with the older couple and regarded them as her family.

In early 1987, the homecare nurse began the process of insuring Deana. The young woman accompanied her but showed little interest in the proceedings, though she answered various questions about her health. On 1st April 1987, Virginia returned alone and paid for the policy: if Deana died, Virginia's son, James, would benefit to the tune of $35,000. Virginia had told the insurance people that James was soon to become Deana's fiancé, though Deana had described him to her mother as a friend.

The following day, Virginia suggested that BJ should drive herself and Deana to the cliffs at Big Sur for a picnic. The threesome enjoyed strolling between the boulders and took photographs of each other in which they all looked happy and relaxed.

Shortly afterwards, however, Virginia contacted Search and Rescue to say that she and her husband had gone back to the car because they were cold, after which Deana had slipped in her high heels and fallen over the cliff. Rescuers soon located her, but she was dead.

Drugged

The autopsy showed that Deana had no alcohol in her system but she did have the components of a prescription drug, Elavil, used to treat depression, and it could have made her weak and drowsy. BJ had a prescription for the drug as it helped him sleep.

Strangely, the young woman's fingers were bruised and her nails broken, as if she'd clung on to the cliff edge and someone had stood on her hands to force her to let go.

There were also inconsistencies in Virginia's story. She'd said that they'd pulled over in the car to take photos of the sunset, and that this was when Deana fell to her death. But she'd fallen at around 4 p.m., and the sun sets later than that in April in California.

Several months later, Deana's mother contacted

a local lawyer called Steve Keeney in Louisville because her insurance company wouldn't pay for the funeral until the coroner had issued the death certificate, but the coroner was still looking into the death.

Keeney examined Virginia's past and discovered that several of her relatives had died in mysterious circumstances whilst alone with Virginia, and her first husband had described her propensity for violence and how he'd woken to find the house ablaze whilst Virginia stood watching the flames from the safety of the lawn. The police were also unhappy with the circumstances surrounding Deana's death and were putting together a case.

Arrest and trial

A few months after Deana's death, BJ and Virginia separated and were soon divorced, but police tracked them down to their new abodes and arrested them. Virginia went on to share a cell for months with Betty Broderick, a woman scorned who murdered her ex-husband and his new wife because she resented their happiness.

Meanwhile, an ex-girlfriend of Virginia's son came forward with a chilling tale. Apparently, Virginia had told her son that BJ was supposed to push Deana over the cliff but she'd fought back valiantly and Virginia had had to help throw her over the precipice.

In late November 1991, jury selection finally began. The following month, BJ died in hospital of Aids so was spared his day in court. The defence said that the then-fifty-year-old practical nurse had been a victim of unfortunate circumstances, that a combination of high winds and high heels had led to Deana's fatal fall.

The defence produced witnesses that spoke of the girl's marijuana use – they hoped that this would make the jury see her as a girl who might also have taken Elavil of her own volition. They noted that three of her boyfriends had been ex-cons, giving jurors the impression that she liked to live dangerously.

In contrast, the prosecution witnesses described her as a lonely girl who missed her ex-husband and was considering a reconciliation, and Virginia McGinnis had described her as being like a friendly puppy who just wanted to be liked. The prosecution showed the snapshots taken at the scene, lingering on one where BJ had his hand on Deana. He was looking at the highway, as if to check that the coast was clear. The jury, having observed Virginia for two months, thought that she was equally culpable and some had privately nicknamed her the Ice Lady.

On 2nd March 1992, they returned with their

verdict: guilty of first-degree murder, conspiracy, insurance fraud and forgery. The defendant stared straight ahead, emotionless as ever. Later, she was sentenced to life without the possibility of parole.

10   Edna Chubb

The following case, that of Edna Chubb, understandably elicited public sympathy. Edna was a hard-working nurse who also had an intolerable number of domestic and financial demands made on her. Eventually she snapped and murdered her sister-in-law.

A strained friendship

Throughout the 1950s, Edna Chubb lived with her husband Ernest in a council house in Broadstairs. She had a heavy workload, caring for the couple's five children (the eldest of whom had a hole in the heart) and her own disabled mother. It was a workload that increased when Ernest's unmarried sister, Lilian Chubb, arrived for a week and ended up staying for the next seven years.

Ernest hoped that the women would become firm friends and Edna did her best to make this happen, but Lilian was not the easiest of guests. She watched Edna do all of the housework, cooking and gardening and never offered to help in any way and she only contributed a small sum towards her lodging, despite the fact that she could have afforded to pay more.

Unable to make ends meet, Edna took a series of part-time cleaning and factory jobs. From October 1955 to January 1958 – a few days before the murder – she also worked twelve-hour nursing shifts at Haine Hospital, Ramsgate. The hospital matron noticed that Mrs Chubb was living on her nerves and was on the verge of a breakdown, but she never took her stress out on the patients and the matron described her as a 'ministering angel of the night'.

The murder

On 6th February 1958, Edna's sister-in-law sat and enjoyed a leisurely breakfast whilst she listened to Edna racing around the house, tidying the bedrooms, making the beds and starting the washing-up in the kitchen. Eventually Lilian put a dirty coffee cup down on the counter that Edna had just cleaned. Lilian then got up to go – and Edna followed her into the hallway and grabbed hold of her scarf from the back, twisting it hard and pulling the woman backwards. Miss Chubb's head hit the wall and she began to make noises, sounds that Mrs Chubb instinctively silenced by putting her hand over the badly injured woman's mouth. The noises ceased, whereupon Mrs Chubb realised that her relative was dead. She remained in shock for a few minutes then fetched a wheelchair they kept in the garden and wheeled the still-warm corpse to the garden shed.

The following day, she waited until her husband had left for work then pushed the body into a hedge by the roadside, where it was discovered almost immediately.

At first, Edna Chubb expressed surprise that her sister-in-law had been murdered, and said that the woman didn't have any enemies. But inquiries showed that Lilian Chubb hadn't left the house on the day of her death, and the police noted that the marks on her neck were sufficiently slight as to have been caused by another woman. When Edna was questioned further she admitted that she'd tugged at the woman's scarf in a moment of rage, but that the death had been an accident.

The trial

In May 1958, Edna pleaded not guilty at the Old Bailey. The defence noted that her workload had been so great that she often survived on two hours' sleep. Witnesses testified that she was a woman without malice. In turn, the prosecution alleged that the victim's neck had been compressed for some considerable time.

Edna Chubb broke down when she took the stand, but admitted that she'd wanted to give her undesirable guest 'a shaking'. After the incident, her sister-in-law had been blue in the face.

The jury acquitted her of murder but returned a verdict of manslaughter, for which she was sentenced to four years' imprisonment. Whilst she was serving out this sentence, her disabled daughter died.

11   Noreen O'Conner

This largely forgotten murder, and its genteel murderess, must be one of the strangest in living memory.

A dedicated carer

Noreen was a staff nurse at the London Clinic but later went into private nursing care in Somerset, looking after a wealthy elderly gentleman. She accompanied him to cricket matches and equestrian events, though her own first love was the Church. As a thank you for providing him with such excellent care, he bought her a beautiful detached limestone house, called Gardeen, in the Somerset village of Loxton.

After his death, 44-year-old Noreen offered a room in the house to a then 75-year-old woman,

Marie Buls, who'd had a live-in position as a maid but now required both accommodation and nursing care. The two spinsters lived happily together and became good friends.

Noreen's life continued to centre around religion and she often raised funds for the local church. She sang religious songs and studied the Bible and began to encourage her friends to sing hymns when they went out on trips.

On 31st August 1954, she told an acquaintance that her dead employer was guiding her from a supposed afterlife. She added, 'the evil spirit is dead for ever,' and concluded, 'if we trust in God, all will be well.' She also sang the first line of a hymn. He was alarmed by her zealousness and concluded that she was mentally ill.

As 31st August moved into the 1st September, the nurse's religious fervour reached its peak. She thought that she felt evil vibrations emanating from the wireless and believed that she heard doors opening and closing. Concerned for her patient, she hurried upstairs and went into Marie's bedroom, took a seat at her bedside and began to hold her hand and pray. She would later say that she prayed for a long time, doubtless to Marie's increasing terror, but she believed that evil had entered her patient's eyes and determined that she must pluck the offending orbs out of the woman's head.

Noreen attempted to do so and a terrible struggle followed, in which Maria rolled out of bed and onto the floor. Her right hand was badly bruised and she lost a tooth as she tried to fight off the younger woman. Her attacker also tore at her lip and at her nostrils before tearing her eyelids and gouging out her eyeballs. Shortly afterwards, the 77-year-old died of blood loss and shock.

Afterwards, the 46-year-old nurse would have no memory of the rest of the night, but, in the morning, she concluded that the evil had left the building. She phoned a friend of the family and said that Marie had become possessed, that he must come to Gardeen immediately. Meanwhile, the housekeeper approached the house and was surprised to see that the upstairs curtains were still closed as Noreen was such an early riser. She let herself into the kitchen and began to prepare breakfast for the two women, but before she could go upstairs, the nurse entered the room, still in her dressing gown, and said that something terrible had happened. She refused to elaborate and the housekeeper assumed that the older woman had had another stroke.

When the family friend, Peter Tiarks, arrived at the house, he found Noreen O'Conner in a trance-like state. She said that she'd seen evil in Marie's eyes, an evil that had become so malevolent she'd plucked both orbs out. Peter asked if she had killed Marie and she replied, 'Well, I suppose she is dead but I did not kill her.' The horrified man called a doctor, who entered the blood spattered bedroom and confirmed that Marie Buls had been murdered in the early hours.

Taken to Weston-super-Mare Police Station and charged, Noreen began to spout religious cant and continued to do so for several hours, becoming violent when officers tried to put her in one of the cells. By the following morning, when she appeared at the local magistrates court, she was calm and polite, entering a not guilty plea.

At the hearing, held at Somerset Assizes, Noreen's solicitor suggested that Marie could have fallen out of bed and died of a stroke and that her eyes were removed by the nurse post-mortem, but magistrates decided they had enough evidence to go to trial and Noreen appeared at Wells Assizes on 15th October that year. Psychiatrists who had assessed her whilst she was in Holloway Prison said that Noreen was in a state of 'acute mania' and didn't know right from wrong. She was found 'guilty but insane' and sentenced to remain at Broadmoor for an indefinite period.

The nurse bowed to the judge before she was taken to the mental health prison, where she remained for the next 29 years before dying of natural causes.

PART TWO

KILLER ON THE WARD

The ward-based killer, especially if he or she works with seriously ill or elderly patients, can claim numerous victims before falling under suspicion. Such killers are often superficially confident but this hides deep feelings of inadequacy and an inability to maintain a lasting, loving relationship. These killers have often been violent towards their significant others and have also been cruel to their pets. Most homicidal nurses deny their crimes: only Charles Cullen, a man who had spent years in therapy and felt comfortable in a confessional capacity, admitted to being a healthcare serial killer.

12 Colin Norris

This Scottish nurse apparently murdered his elderly female patients because he hated them, but it's unclear why he took such drastic action rather than retrain for a different career.

Divorce

Colin Norris was born in Glasgow on the 12th February 1976 to June and Colin Norris. June was a typist, whilst Colin senior worked as a painter and decorator. The nuclear family lived in Partick and little Colin was a happy and lively child. He joined the boy scouts and, as one of his projects, helped learning-disabled people. He also loved amateur dramatics or anything else that put him centre stage.

His mother and father separated when he was

seven and his mother won custody. By the time he was nine, the divorce was finalised. He then became even closer to his maternal grandmother, who doted on him and who lived in the next street. At thirteen, his mother remarried. His father, who he saw infrequently, also married again.

Colin wasn't particularly gifted academically but left school with six standard examinations (the equivalent of six GCSEs) and began to study Travel at college. After a year of this, he left to become a travel agent. In the same time frame, when he was around seventeen, he allegedly stole money from his elderly relatives at a family funeral and his father was so disgusted by this behaviour that he broke off contact with him. Later, when the older man got back in touch, Colin demanded £18,000 compensation for being the child of a broken home. His father was shocked at this request and they became estranged for a second time.

After six years working in the travel industry, Colin Norris decided to retrain as a nurse, telling friends that this would allow him to 'make a difference' to society. He began studying for a Higher Nursing Diploma at Dundee University in September 1998, and was given a placement at the School of Nursing and Midwifery, but he clashed with his personal tutor as he always thought he knew best and hated being told what to do. He would later quip to police that, 'It was a personality clash. I had a personality and she didn't.' But the truth was very different, as he fought with everyone in authority. He would later be described by the judge and by the press as 'lazy' but he had two part-time jobs to support himself during his student years and had never been unemployed.

Colin was gay and sometimes brought men back to his student accommodation to spend the night. He appeared to be comfortable with his sexuality. He was also supremely confident at work, bordering on being smug.

In January 1999, he attended a lecture on diabetes and, that May, he did some of his nurse's training at Dundee's well-regarded Ninewells Hospital and learnt more about diabetes care. His placement ended in July, after which he moved to the Royal Victoria Hospital, also in Dundee, to continue his training. He worked on the geriatric ward and hated it. He told his tutor that he loathed elderly people, and he often took unauthorised days off.

In September, he attended another lecture about diabetic management, which included information about using insulin and, in January 2001, he went to a lecture about a female nurse who had been accused of murdering elderly patients by injecting them with the drug. Later that year, he did part of his nurse's training at a nursing home in Dundee but hated changing sheets and dirty clothing and admitted to a friend that he loathed working with geriatric patients. He fulfilled only a few days of his four-week placement then phoned in and claimed to have a sore throat for the rest of the month.

In June 2001, Norris graduated with a Higher Nursing Diploma and, that autumn, began working as a staff nurse at Leeds General Infirmary. He also worked at St James Hospital in the city, assisting in the orthopaedic ward.

Colin Norris now thought of himself as an authority figure and a medical specialist and was enraged at being expected to do basic patient care, so when an octogenarian asked him to empty his catheter, Norris refused and told him to do it himself. The 87-year-old man attempted to follow his instructions but fell and was deeply distressed. When another patient fell out of bed, two elderly women called to Norris for assistance and he told one of them, 'I hope you suffer,' and said to the other, 'Rot in hell.' As a result of this and similar incidents, his dislike of senior citizens, especially females, was well known on the ward.

Ironically, one of his allotted tasks was to wash the vaginas of elderly women, some of whom had bladder infections and were incontinent. He found the smell intolerable. Most people would have reassured themselves that they'd soon be able to move out of geriatric nursing and into a specialism that held more appeal for them, or else they would have left the profession altogether. However, according to the police, Colin Norris decided to eliminate the most difficult patients rather than change his job...

Attempted murder

On 2nd May 2001, at Leeds General Hospital, Colin nursed ninety-year-old Vera Wilby, who had been left with a broken hip after a fall. Surgeons set her hip, but her condition deteriorated. That May, police would later allege, Colin Norris administered morphine to make her sleepy, followed by further drugs. His shift ended and he left the hospital, whereupon other nurses found her semi-conscious and suffering from hypoglycaemia. They stabilised her and she survived. (She died in a nursing home a year later from natural causes.)

Four murders

The following month, eighty-year-old Doris Ludlam arrived on Norris's ward, also suffering from a broken hip. Thirteen days later, according to the police, Colin gave her double the recommended dose of diamorphine to make her sleepy, followed by insulin to reduce her blood sugar levels. Forty-five minutes after his shift ended, she was discovered in a coma and, two days later, she died.

Another of Colin's patients, Bridget Bourke, aged 88, had numerous health problems including complications following a stroke and a chronic bacterial infection. On 21st July, he raised the alarm, saying that he'd found her unconscious. Tests showed that she was hypoglycaemic despite not suffering from diabetes. The following day she died and the cause of death was recorded as a stroke.

In October, Colin worked the night shift at a different Leeds hospital, St James's, and nursed 79-year-old Irene Crookes, who had been admitted with a fractured hip and breathing difficulties. Nine days after being admitted, she was found unconscious and hypoglycaemic. She died the next day.

The following month, Colin's patients included Ethel Hall, aged 86, who was admitted to Leeds General Hospital for a fractured hip. Five days later, she was making good progress and had been walking about the ward, so a nurse was surprised when Colin Norris said that he didn't like the look of her. He added that people always died when he was on night shift and said that things most often went wrong at about 5.15 a.m.

At 5 a.m., a nurse found Ethel choking and slumped down in her bed. She called for another nurse and they lifted her up, cleaned her airways and checked her blood sugar, finding that her glucose levels were so low that her brain had shut down. Tests revealed that her insulin levels were twelve times the normal limit, a dose too high to have ever been given accidentally. She remained in a coma. Belatedly aware that they had a potential killer on the ward, the hospital called the police.

West Yorkshire Police began their investigation on 6th December 2002. On the 11th, Ethel Hall died without ever having regained consciousness and her husband of fifty years was so distraught that he had a heart attack three weeks after her death, after which he remained in a weakened state. Norris was interviewed, as were all of the other doctors and nurses, and told police that he'd been unlucky for the past twelve months. He was arrested and suspended from work. However, even though they interviewed him at length, the police didn't have enough to charge him, and he was released, moving back to Glasgow and taking a job with an events company – work that included foreign travel.

The following September, detectives arranged for Mrs Bourke's body to be exhumed and tested. The pathologist reported that she had died from an insulin-induced coma – in other words, the killer had claimed another victim. Critics later wondered why the hospital's insulin stocks weren't more carefully managed, why no one noticed that phials of the medicine had disappeared.

Meanwhile, Colin Norris went on a cruise as part of his job and began a relationship with another traveller. The man would later allege that Colin had thrown a bottle at him during one argument, and hit him on the head during another row.

Whilst the former nurse sailed the Seven Seas, West Yorkshire Police continued their investigations. They found that Colin Norris had worked at two hospitals in the city and that there had been seventy-two deaths during that time, eighteen of which were suspicious. By poring over the record books, they were able to ascertain which nurses had been working with which patients and who had had the opportunity to be alone with these patients before they died. Colin Norris had worked the night shift or weekend shifts when eight of the patients became hypoglycaemic, shifts when senior staff weren't on duty. He admitted that he was the last medic to see them before they took a turn for the worse. Detectives decided to charge him with the murders of Ethel Hall, Doris Ludlam, Bridget Bourke and Irene Crookes and with the attempted murder of Vera Wilby.

Arrest

Norris was convinced that the police would not proceed whilst they had purely circumstantial evidence, so he was visibly shocked on 12th October 2005 when they charged him with four counts of murder and one of attempted murder. He said that patients always made a noise or asked what was going on when a nurse injected them, so how had he managed to do so without drawing attention to himself? The police, however, believe that he had given them drugs to make them drowsy first. Colin admitted telling another nurse that patients' conditions always worsened at about 5.15 a.m. and that Ethel Hall had deteriorated at 5 a.m., but now said to detectives, 'I'm no Mystic Meg.'

The motive

Police noted that Colin could be charismatic and quite funny on occasion but, at other times, he was overwhelmingly arrogant and aggressive. They were convinced that he'd murdered the women simply because they irritated him.

Psychiatrist Dr Richard Badcock came to the same conclusion after studying the case, stating that Norris appeared to be a psychopath who killed patients who got in his way. The ones who were murdered had needed their clothing or bedding changed, tasks that he abhorred.

Trial

On 16th October 2005, he went on trial at Newcastle Crown Court, charged with four murders and one attempted murder. He was convinced that he would be found innocent. The media would later report that he attacked the press, but it was a minor act of aggression where he lightly pushed a press photographer out of the way.

The jury returned on 3rd March 2008 and he was convicted by an eleven-to-one majority. He showed no emotion at the verdict, though his mother later said that he was shell-shocked and that, if he'd been tried in his native Scotland, the jury would surely have returned with a Not Proven verdict. Given a thirty-year minimum sentence, he was sent to Durham Prison where the other prisoners nicknamed him Dr Death. Later that year, lawyers announced his plans to appeal.

Struck off

In April 2009, the Nursing and Midwifery Council held a hearing at which Colin Norris appeared via a web link from prison. He claimed that he was innocent of all of the charges but the council took just five minutes to ban him from ever working in a nursing capacity again.

13   Kristen Gilbert

With her love of medical emergencies and Munchausen's syndrome tendencies, this American nurse shared some personality traits with Britain's Beverly Allitt. With Munchausen's, the sufferer hurts him or herself (or pretends to) in order to elicit sympathy from friends, family and medical practitioners. With Munchausen's syndrome by proxy, the person harms others, often children, in order to become the centre of attention, sometimes with lethal results.

A desperate need for attention

Kristen was born on the 15th November 1967 to Claudia and Richard Strickland. Her father was in the services at the time of her birth but later pursued a career as an electronics engineer and her mother was a teacher. When she was six months old the family relocated to Fall River, Massachusetts.

When Kristen was three they enrolled her in a strict day care centre and, when she was seven, her parents had a second girl. Kristen resented the newcomer and now spent more time with her maternal grandmother and grandfather. She seemed desperate for attention and often invented stories, sometimes of a dramatic nature. She also told her school friends that she was related to Lizzie Borden, who'd been acquitted in Fall River in 1892 of murdering her parents with an axe.

The teenager had a high IQ and, by sixteen, was taking a pre-med course at college. With her high energy and pretty features, she went on lots of dates but her boyfriends always ended the relationship, finding that she was unstable and violent. Enraged at their rejection, she would vandalise their houses or their cars.

Suicidal

In 1986 Kristen met Glen Gilbert and, in 1988, she married him. But, during an argument a month after the honeymoon, she attacked him with a knife. At other times she turned the violence inwards and attempted suicide. Glen was initially very much in love with her but found that she was constantly dissatisfied, buying clothes and household goods that she couldn't afford and evidencing an almost pathological need to show off, even claiming that she was from a wealthy family.

Unexpected deaths

The following year, Kristen graduated and began working as a registered nurse at the Veteran Affairs Medical Center (abbreviated to VAMC) in Massachusetts. She was so well read on medical affairs and drug use that other nurses often went to her for advice.

However, everyone was surprised early in 1990 when one of Kristen's patients died; this started a pattern of unexpected cardiac arrests and her colleagues began to jokingly call Kristen the 'Angel of Death'. It took an alert clerical worker to spot that Kristen had three times the death rate of any other nurse in the VAMC. The clerical worker confided her fears in a supervisor but was told to go away and stop making false accusations.

That same year, Kristen gave birth to a son, but, two months later, returned to work, doing the 4 p.m.-to-midnight shift. One day, when everything was quiet, she reported that she'd answered the phone and that a voice had warned there was a bomb in the hospital. Everyone had to be evacuated until police searched the building. Kristen was in the midst of the drama and seemed enlivened and excited by it.

On another occasion, Kristen informed her startled co-workers that she'd found a suspicious-looking package in a hospital cupboard, a box with a swastika drawn on the front. Kristen told her supervisor that it probably contained a bomb – but the bomb squad found that it was merely a wrapped-up box of tissues. Still, it added excitement to an otherwise humdrum day.

Even more alarmingly, the Gilberts' pets always died mysteriously. Kristen would later say that she'd taken one dog to the vets to be put down, but this turned out not to be true.

In November 1993, the couple had a second son and their already shaky marriage deteriorated further, so that, by 1994, Kristen was telling her colleagues that she wanted a divorce. By 1995, she'd lost weight, was dressing more sexily and began to flirt with James Perrault, the hospital's young security guard. In the autumn of that year they became lovers, having sex in his car.

Shortly after this, Glen became very sick. He was taken to hospital and found to have very low potassium levels, almost unheard of in a man of his age.

On 21st August 1995, the medical team at VAMC stabilised veteran Stanley Jagodowski. Shortly afterwards, Kristen was seen entering his room with a syringe, but she soon hurried out, leaving the Korean veteran shouting that his arm hurt. A few minutes later, he went into cardiac arrest. He was resuscitated and put on a life support machine but died without regaining consciousness. On 1st December, Kristen left her husband and children and moved into her own apartment, a move that made it easier for her to see her lover. At work, her patients continued to die. A 35-year-old schizophrenic was admitted suffering from flu but suddenly went into a fatal cardiac arrest, and an army veteran almost died in suspicious circumstances. Meanwhile, someone had been using phials of epinephrine, an overdose of which can prove lethal to a healthy heart.

Sometimes one of Kristen's patients would die unexpectedly, allowing her to leave work early to be with her boyfriend, James Perrault. When phoning the relatives to report the death, she was frequently callous, reporting 'your husband has passed away' then abruptly hanging up. (Harold Shipman was equally callous towards the newly bereaved.)

Once when she injected a patient, he began to scream that his arm was burning and managed to attract the attention of other medics. They saved him after he went into cardiac arrest. When he regained consciousness, he told them that his chest had begun to feel heavy after Nurse Kristen Gilbert injected something into his IV line.

An investigation

The police were called in and special agents began investigating. In time, they suspected her of forty murders. They exhumed Stanley Jagodowski's body and found abnormally high levels of epinephrine. They also exhumed the body of another patient, Ed Skwira, and found a similarly lethal dose. Two of her other patients, Henry Hudon and Kenny Cutting, had also died of excessive epinephrine. At Kristen's apartment, they found epinephrine, which she explained away by saying that she was allergic to bee stings – but her medical notes showed that she was only allergic to penicillin. Later, she became so violent towards James (who now wanted nothing more to do with her) and her ex-husband that she was admitted to a psychiatric hospital. When she was released, she broke into James's home and he had her arrested and took out a restraining order against her. Sometime later she claimed that she'd taken a massive overdose of aspirin and was again admitted for psychiatric evaluation, staff finding her manipulative and untruthful. She took a third overdose in August 1996, but survived.

Chaos

Kristen Gilbert continued to cause chaos, making numerous hang-up and heavy-breathing calls to James and vandalising his car. Every nurse who had spoken to the investigators also found their property damaged. Equally damning, someone – disguising their voice with a Talkgirl toy that changes the tone – made phone calls to her former workplace claiming that another bomb had been left. Detectives investigated and found that Kristen had bought a Talkgirl the previous day, yet she seemed unable to recognise the gravity of her situation, telling a friend that someday this would make a good film.

She was charged with making the phone calls, pleaded not guilty and was ordered to be electronically tagged. She also had to live at her parents' house and was prohibited from going out.

Bomb threats trial

As her trial for making the bomb threats neared, Kristen was subject to an in-depth psychological evaluation, which determined that she suffered from Narcissistic Personality Disorder, Obsessive Compulsive Personality Traits and Antisocial Personality Disorder. Psychiatrists noted that she made light of all of her problems and even denied her documented suicidal acts.

The jury listened to the tape that had been played down the hospital telephone line, deliberated and found her guilty. Kristen was sentenced to fifteen months and sent to a federal prison in Connecticut.

Murder trial

On 20th November 2000, Kristen's trial began. (As in almost all cases of multiple murder, the defendant was only tried for a few representative cases.) She pleaded not guilty to all of the charges. The defence said that she was a good wife and mother whose marriage had broken down under the strain of doing shift work. They tried to put the blame on some of her colleagues who were using recreational drugs.

The prosecution, however, produced numerous

witnesses who had seen the registered nurse acting strangely. A nurse took the stand and described seeing Kristen entering a patient's room with a syringe when he had not been scheduled to receive any medication. Another nurse had seen a patient scream 'She did it!' and point at Kristen as he collapsed. Kristen had also exhibited a level of Munchausen's syndrome and had been treated for twenty-two injuries during her years at work. Kristen's ex-husband and ex-boyfriend both took the stand to say that she had confessed to them whilst the investigation was underway.

On 14th March 2001, the jury found Kristen guilty of the first-degree murder of three veterans, namely Ed Skwira, Kenny Cutting and Henry Hudon. She was found guilty of the second-degree murder of veteran Stanley Jagodowski and found guilty of the attempted murder of veterans Angelo Vella and Thomas Callahan. The jury acquitted her of the death of Francis Marier. (First-degree murder is an intentional killing by deliberate and premeditated action, whereas second-degree murder is a homicide committed whilst perpetrating a felony.) She sobbed as they read out their verdict. The judge subsequently sentenced her to four consecutive life terms. Two months later she began serving out her life sentence in a women's prison in Fort Worth, Texas.

Kristen appealed, but withdrew this when the US Supreme Court ruled that prosecutors could pursue the death penalty. She now spends her days reading and quilting and proclaiming her innocence.

14   Robert Diaz

This nurse claimed that he had psychic powers that told him, who would die next on his ward – in reality, he was killing the patients himself.

Early hell

Robert Diaz was born in Indiana in 1938, one of sixteen children. The family was desperately poor and Robert suffered from several serious illnesses throughout his difficult childhood. It's possible that the time he spent in hospital awakened in him the desire to become a doctor, and he told everyone that he'd become a medic when he grew up. But his illnesses resulted in him missing out on study time and, after a total of only ten years of schooling, the teenager dropped out and took a job in the same car factory as several of his relatives.

At eighteen, in a bid to get away, he joined the Marine Corps, but he went AWOL and was later discharged; his exciting new life was over. Crestfallen, he returned to Indiana and resumed his factory job.

Over time, Robert became enamoured of the supernatural, convinced that he could tap into the energies of so-called demons and that they would grant him the power and happiness he could not find in his everyday life. He also believed in reincarnation, Egyptian sorcery and psychic powers.

Robert married in 1961 and fathered five children. He continued to be a weak thinker, convinced that, if he stared at the family cat for long enough, he would establish a psychic link with her and could control her mind. (In reality, cats find being stared at very threatening so he doubtless unsettled the poor animal.) No one was surprised when he and his wife got divorced in 1972.

Robert now took stock of his life and decided to train as a vocational nurse, getting good grades. After he graduated, he insisted that his friends and relatives call him Dr Diaz. He retained his delusions of grandeur and interest in the occult, telling anyone who would listen that he had been a member of the Egyptian royal family in a previous life.

The new nurse

Quietly spoken and bespectacled, Robert found it easy to obtain employment and was soon nursing part-time in two Los Angeles hospitals, namely the Community Hospital of the Valleys in Perris, California, and San Gorgonio Pass Memorial Hospital in Banning. However, shortly after his arrival in March 1981, the death toll at the Community Hospital began to rise.

His behaviour also caused concern, as he sometimes told the other nurses that a healthy-looking patient was going to die, claiming that he could read the person's aura. Chillingly, he was never wrong.

In April, an anonymous female caller contacted the coroner of San Bernardino County in Los Angeles and said that nineteen mysterious deaths had occurred in the Perris hospital. The coroner reported this to the police and they, in turn, contacted the hospital. The latter confirmed that eleven patients had died suddenly and all had exhibited an unusually high level of blood acidity. Many of their files had disappeared from the intensive care unit and suspicion fell on one of their newest nurses, Robert Diaz, who had access to the files and who had predicted the deaths at times when the patients were stable or even on the road to recovery. Moreover, another sudden death had occurred at the memorial hospital, where he also worked part-time.

Detectives spoke to the nurse's colleagues and some admitted seeing him carry out unauthorised injections. This gave police the opening they needed to search Robert's home, where they found morphine, the heart drug lidocaine (his murder weapon of choice) and syringes pre-filled with the drug. These syringes were marked as containing 2% of lidocaine, whereas tests showed that they contained 20% – enough to bring on cardiac arrest. Robert said that he'd mistakenly brought the syringes home in his shirt pocket but he couldn't explain why they'd been tampered with. The authorities now began the unpleasant process of exhuming and autopsying his patients.

Arrested

In November 1981, Robert Diaz was arrested and charged with twelve murders, and responded by issuing a legal suit claiming defamation of character, which was dismissed by the court. He said that doctors hadn't responded promptly to medical emergencies and that was why so many patients died. All that he'd done, he claimed, was take over the doctor's duties on occasion to try and save a patient's life.

His ex-wife initially backed him up but, when she saw the evidence against him, she accepted the likelihood of his guilt. There had been less than one death per month at the Perris hospital in the year before Diaz joined the staff, yet, during his three-and-a-half weeks of employment, there had been seventeen deaths, fourteen of which were under the new nurse's direct care.

Diaz opted for a bench trial rather than face a jury of his peers. The prosecution alleged that the murders had made him feel powerful, more like the surgeon or doctor that he desperately wanted to be, but this was supposition as Diaz refused to admit his guilt so couldn't talk about the motive behind the deaths. The defence failed to find a single character witness for the nurse, who, in March 1984, was found guilty of all twelve murders. His legal team asked the judge to spare his life but he was sentenced to death. Now in his seventies, Robert remains on Death Row at San Quentin and – given how seldom state executions are actually carried out in the prison – will most likely die of natural causes in due course.

PART THREE

MEDICS IN THE MEDIA

Some doctors who kill receive comparatively little media attention, perhaps only generating local news interest for the murder of a spouse or child. But the following killers were very much in the spotlight, partly because of the number of their alleged victims, and partly because they targeted vulnerable groups such as children and the elderly, causing a public outcry. Although most of these killers looked uncomfortable whilst facing reporters, Orville Lynn Majors actually courted the TV networks in a bid to proclaim his innocence.

15   Dr Harold Shipman

Harold Frederick Shipman, an outwardly mild-looking family man, would go on to become Britain's most prolific known healthcare killer.

A sad childhood

Harold was born on the 14th January 1946 to Vera and Harold Shipman, who lived on a council estate in Nottingham. His mother was a housewife, his father a lorry driver. They soon decided that it would be easier to refer to their first son by his middle name, and this was invariably shortened to Freddie and, later, Fred. The couple already had a seven-year-old daughter and, four years after Fred's birth, went on to have another son.

The family lived in a council house but Vera

wanted more for her children and soon pinned her hopes on Fred, the shyest and most sensitive of her children, but he was left-handed and struggled to learn to write, as teachers in those days tried to force such children to use their right hand.

Vera didn't like him playing in the street with the other local boys, so, in the evenings, he stayed at home with her or went out running on his own. He showed prowess on the sports field and enjoyed going to football matches with his father, but was equally happy spending time on his own.

His mother told him repeatedly that he was special and encouraged him to study hard and, by dint of hard work rather than academic aptitude, he made it to the local grammar school. Sixty per cent of the boys there were from similar working-class backgrounds so he didn't feel like an outsider, though he was never particularly sociable.

Sadly, by Fred's mid-teens, Vera was suffering from lung cancer and soon her only relief was when the GP arrived and administered an injection of morphine. Fred cared for her every evening when he came home from school. He watched, distraught, as she grew thinner and weaker, finally taking permanently to her bed. On the evening of Friday, 21st June 1963, her pain again dulled by opiates, she died. Seventeen-year-old Fred was so distressed that he went out in the rain and ran for hours, essentially self-medicating by creating a runner's high. By now he had decided that he wanted to be a GP.

Shipman went to Leeds University to study Medicine and met a teenager called Primrose on the bus. She was on her way to college, where she was studying Art and Design. Primrose had grown up in a repressive Methodist household and wasn't allowed to go to the cinema or the youth club. Instead, her life revolved around Sunday school and church. She and Fred began dating and, within months, she was pregnant. That same year, in November 1966, they married and, the following February became parents of a baby girl.

Shipman had just turned twenty-one yet had to support a seventeen-year-old wife and newborn child and continue his studies, all on a modest student grant. To cope, he began to take larger and larger doses of pethidine, a painkiller with morphine-like qualities, which he had first tried when taking part in a medical trial. It would have prevented the tension headaches, stomach pains and general weariness that many medical students experience as they study long into the night.

Unlike many of his fellow students, he did not

become queasy when attending autopsies and, instead, seemed fascinated by the corpses. At this stage in his life, he'd probably only seen two naked bodies – his wife's and his own – so his curiosity was understandable.

The young medic passed his exams in 1970 and moved his little family to Pontefract, where he was a junior houseman at the local infirmary. At this stage, Shipman's regular injections of pethidine would still have been creating a euphoric state, making him feel detached from the everyday pressures of life.

The following April, the couple had their first son. Fred stayed on at Pontefract Infirmary for another two years, earning qualifications in obstetrics and gynaecology, but he really wanted to be a GP and, in 1974, he moved into general practice, working alongside several other doctors in Todmorden, Yorkshire.

He proved to be a natural, putting in long hours and taking further work home with him. The couple were able to afford a semi-detached house and soon settled into the community.

A growing addiction

By now his dependence on pethidine had reached a dangerously high level, and most of the veins in his arms and legs had collapsed. As a result, he was forced to inject into his groin, the practice of many junkies. Over time, the drug causes neurological symptoms, so he began to have blackouts when he got home from work. On one occasion he passed out whilst having a bath and Primrose was unable to revive him. She called one of the other doctors at his practice and Shipman was sent for tests and wrongly diagnosed with epilepsy. Primrose now chauffeured him to all of his appointments as he was unable to drive.

Months later, his fellow doctors discovered that he'd been prescribing pethidine for numerous patients but actually keeping it for himself; suddenly they understood the real reason for his blackouts. They confronted him and he said that he would get help but would continue to work at the practice. He seemed unaware of how unethical his behaviour had been. When they insisted that they'd get a temporary doctor to come in whilst he went into rehab, he stormed out in a rage. Arrested for drug misuse, he admitted to police that he'd been overworked and depressed, so had been injecting himself with pethidine up to fourteen times a day.

Shipman began to receive treatment whilst awaiting trial – it normally only takes three weeks for the symptoms of pethidine withdrawal to abate.

Unable to work as a doctor or pay his mortgage, he and Primrose gave up their house and took the children to live with her parents. When his case came to court, the magistrate was sympathetic (drug misuse amongst the medical fraternity is not uncommon) and he was fined heavily but spared a custodial sentence. He and his family moved to Darlington, where he worked as a clinical health officer, liaising between GPs and community groups.

However, he wanted to return to GP practice, so was delighted in 1977 when he saw that there was a vacancy in Hyde, Greater Manchester, where he'd be working alongside six other general practitioners. He was honest about his former pethidine abuse and the other GPs agreed that he deserved a second chance. They – and the patients he inherited from the previous incumbent – liked him and he presented himself as being friendly and humorous with an enquiring mind.

Strange days

Superficially, Shipman was very similar to his contemporaries in that he had a semi-detached house with a garden, but Primrose had long ago stopped doing even basic housework so the

Shipmans' home was filthy and rank. Newspapers were piled up in every room and clothes littered the floors. Yet the couple went on to have a third child in March 1979 and a fourth in April 1982, both boys.

Jekyll and Hyde

At home, the doctor was becoming an increasingly irate parent (and Primrose had become clinically obese) but most patients saw a very different side to the doctor, who kept up with the latest medical breakthroughs and was prepared to prescribe expensive medicines for them. He used their first names and asked after their spouses, children and pets. As a result, he had an excellent reputation in the area and there was a year-long wait to get on his list.

Shipman doubtless revelled in the deference that his elderly working-class patients showed him, as this buoyed up his own impression of himself as an important man, yet he was aloof and abrupt with the practice's receptionists and with drug reps, or any other co-worker whom he saw as less educated than himself. And, over time, the other doctors noticed that he had to get his own way at meetings and show his superiority.

Suspicious deaths

By the early Eighties, some of the doctor's patients had begun to die unexpectedly. A sprightly pensioner, for example, was found dead in her chair, ostensibly by Dr Shipman, moments after finishing her lunch. The seventy-year-old had arthritis but was otherwise fit and in very good health. Although the families and friends of many of these elderly ladies were deeply shocked at their sudden demise, there was nothing to alert the medical fraternity to the fact that they might have a serial killer in their midst. (Police believed that she was one of his earlier victims, though he was never charged with causing her death. They would take him to court for only fifteen murders in order to avoid overwhelming the judicial system and the jury.)

As he aged, Shipman became increasingly aloof and cantankerous and, in 1992, moved into a surgery of his own, close to the centre of Hyde. Female patients now began to die on his premises.

An 82-year-old went to the doctor in January 1994, suffering from shoulder pain. Police suspect that Shipman injected her with a fatal dose of diamorphine (all of his victims appeared to have been given lethal injections of drugs, mainly from the morphine family) but he told her friend, waiting outside, that she had keeled over and died as he took her blood pressure. He said that it had been a massive heart attack.

Eighteen months later, one of his 68-year-old patients felt unwell whilst out shopping, so called in to his surgery for a check-up. She, too, apparently succumbed to a massive heart attack.

Later that year, an 87-year-old woman walked to Shipman's for a check-up, reached the surgery and apparently had a stroke, followed, moments later, by another stroke. Again, because of her age, her shocked family accepted the doctor's explanation for her unexpected death.

In May, 1996, a 72-year-old pensioner went to the doctor for her usual three-monthly injection for pernicious anaemia. She had driven to the surgery in her car but left on a covered stretcher bound for the mortuary, much to the distress of her relatives.

A year later, 63-year-old Ivy Lomas took the bus to the doctor's practice in Hyde. She was a regular visitor, often complaining of aches and pains, and it seems that Shipman was tired of her. He later told police that he had put her in the treatment room to rest whilst he attended to three other patients, returning to find her dead. She, too, was listed as having died of a heart attack. In three years, a total of five women died in Shipman's surgery, yet many doctors have never had a single patient die on their premises.

Such deaths would occur in his practice throughout his working life, and a local taxi driver, John Shaw, who drove elderly patients to Shipman's surgery, became increasingly perturbed at the number that suddenly expired.

The visitor

Many more of Shipman's patients died at home, often being found after he'd been seen leaving the property. Others had told friends that they were expecting a home visit from the doctor – but, when they were found dead, he denied having visited them.

Alone in house after house, Harold Shipman helped himself to rings, brooches and necklaces and gave them to Primrose, probably telling her that they were gifts from grateful patients. He also took the contents of the deceased's purses or petty cash tins. On other occasions, he took family heirlooms, leaving the relatives of the deceased to regard each other with suspicion, wondering which of them had taken their mother's coveted china dolls or auntie's jewellery box. Police now believe that by this time Shipman was killing at least one patient every week, sometimes more.

The local undertaker was becoming suspicious as the doctor had a much higher death toll than any other GP in the area. The firm also noted that virtually all of the women had been found sitting upright and fully clothed during the daytime, with only one having died in her nightdress and at night, yet it's much more usual for elderly people to die in bed after a few days or weeks of ill health.

Shipman also used his patients to get more drugs for himself, prescribing large amounts of morphine to a patient called Jim King, supposedly for prostate cancer, but the hospital had written to him to say that their original diagnosis was wrong, that Mr King didn't have the disease – news that Dr Shipman had suppressed. The doctor continued to prescribe morphine for the unfortunate man, turning him into an addict. He also prescribed morphine for those who were terminally ill, but kept some of the drug for himself, using it to kill his healthy and unsuspecting patients, both female and male, though the former predominated.

Meanwhile, the relatives of Shipman's patients were amazed at the speed with which their loved ones had deteriorated. In January 1998, Tony Nuttall returned from work to find that his 64-year-old mother Norah had a persistent cough and had been given medication that morning by the doctor. Tony popped out to do a few chores and when he returned, Shipman met him at the door and said that his mother had chest pains, that he'd called 999. The doctor then pretended to examine his mother further and announced that she was dead, adding that he'd cancel the ambulance. He appeared to make this call but, later, records would show that he hadn't phoned the emergency services.

Shipman pulled a similar stunt with other friends and neighbours, saying that he had booked his ailing patient a hospital bed then pretending to call and cancel it. It made him look like a caring GP, part of a wider medical circle, rather than a serial killer who was acting alone.

On 18th February 1998, he falsified another patient's records, typing the symptoms of a brain tumour into Maureen Ward's medical files. (He was treating her for headaches.) Immediately afterwards, he drove to the 58-year-old's flat and apparently found her dead.

By March 1998, a local doctor who was asked to countersign many of Shipman's death certificates was so alarmed at the death count that he contacted the police. They investigated quietly for three weeks, without alerting Dr Shipman, but could find no motive for murder and decided that the doctor had done nothing wrong.

The killing continues

The doctor continued to kill with impunity. On 11th May 1998, he visited 73-year old Winifred Mellor at her home and gave her a lethal injection, then went to a neighbour, saying that he could see her lying in her chair but that she wasn't answering the door. Upon being given entry, he confirmed her death and, when the neighbour left, stole the contents of Mrs Mellor's purse. She was a deeply religious woman so her priest arrived and Shipman was offhand with him and with the family, telling them that she had had angina. He later falsified his records to create a false history of this disease.

On 12th June 1998, Joan Melia felt that she was coming down with a summer cold and went to the doctor. She was seventy-three but looked much younger and had just come back from an energetic foreign holiday. To her surprise, Shipman said that she was suffering from pneumonia and sent her home. He made an unexpected visit to her house later that afternoon and injected her with his beloved morphine, after which it's likely that he took her life savings; she was known to keep money on the premises but very little was found. Her boyfriend found her dead in her chair at 5 p.m., a cup of tea by her side. He phoned Shipman, who came round and offhandedly confirmed the death.

Shipman often spent time in a patient's flat after

they died. One woman noticed that he was with her 58-year-old neighbour (who had developed breathing difficulties due to a bad cold) for almost an hour. She let herself in after he'd gone and found the patient dead and already cold. Confronted by this information, the doctor said that he'd spent the time trying to convince his patient to go to hospital. In reality, he probably spent it prowling around the house, looking for valuables.

Another woman waited in an upstairs kitchen whilst her friend was downstairs in the lounge being attended to by the doctor. Shipman suddenly walked into the kitchen and was startled to see her there but, after a moment, he recovered his equilibrium and told her that her friend had died of a massive stroke.

Also, a man who called round at his sister's house was in time to see the doctor leaving the house with a sewing machine. Shipman said that his sister had just died but that she'd previously said that he could have the machine for Primrose, his wife.

Forgery

So far, Shipman had apparently been content with stealing cash and trinkets from his victims' houses but now he got greedy. He gave 81-year-old Kathleen Grundy a lethal injection, then forged her will, making him the benefactor of her £400,000 estate.

Kathleen's relatives were immediately suspicious. She'd been in excellent health, could walk for miles and spent most days doing charitable and community work. On 23rd June 1998, she mentioned to friends that she was taking part in a medical trial being run by Dr Shipman and said he was coming to her house to take blood the following day. She'd been found dead by a charity co-worker within hours of the doctor's visit to supposedly take blood, yet he told enquirers that he'd only seen her for a chat.

Even more suspicious was the appearance of her will. She was an educated woman with secretarial training, yet the will was filled with spelling and typing errors. Kathleen had been very close to her family, and her daughter Angela, a solicitor, had always handled her legal affairs, yet the will had been sent to a firm of solicitors in town. The document said that she'd chosen to be cremated but before her death she'd talked of wanting to be buried. Her relatives contested the will and, a month after burial, her corpse was exhumed.

Autopsy

Meanwhile, police went to Shipman's surgery and asked to see his typewriter. 'Kathleen Grundy borrows it,' he said as he handed it over, clearly keen to explain why Kathleen's will had been typed on his machine. Tests indeed showed that the will had been typed on the machine, though Kathleen's fingerprints weren't on it – but Shipman's were. One of his fingerprints was also found on the will, a document that had supposedly gone straight from Kathleen to the solicitors in town.

Shipman now started to tell anyone who would listen that Kathleen had been an intravenous drug user. He falsified her medical records to suggest a history of suspected drug use, but computer experts were able to show when these bogus entries had been made.

The doctor continued to practise, though he offered at least some of his patients the option of seeing another medic. He broke down on two or three occasions when discussing Kathleen Grundy's suspicious death with them, but he remained arrogant when dealing with police officers, making it clear that he regarded them as inferior beings.

A murder inquiry

On 2nd September, the toxicology reports came back, confirming that there was a large amount of morphine in Kathleen Grundy's system. Shipman had been careless in his choice of drug – many disappear from the body within days, but morphine can remain in the tissues for centuries. Somewhat alarmingly, he was allowed to continue his surgery until Monday 7th, when he was arrested.

The authorities continued to exhume Shipman's patients. Another eleven graves were opened and large amounts of morphine were found in the corpses. Questioned further by police in October 1998, Shipman realised that he was going to jail for a very long time and became so upset that he suffered a kind of psychological collapse, apparently crawling about on the police station floor and becoming incoherent. He was charged with three murders and sent to prison, where he was put on suicide watch. Later, he was charged with another twelve murders, though police were convinced that there were dozens more.

Meanwhile, Shipman responded to the antidepressants that the prison doctor prescribed for him, and he began to write frequent ungrammatical stream-of-consciousness letters to various acquaintances. In one letter, he said that he'd retire completely from medicine if he was cleared.

Trial

His trial opened at Preston Crown Court on 5th October 1999. He was accused of killing fifteen women, namely Kathleen Grundy, Joan Melia,

Winifred Mellor, Bianka Pomfret, Marie Quinn, Ivy Lomas, Irene Turner, Jean Lilley, Muriel Grimshaw, Marie West, Kathleen Wagstaff, Pamela Hillier, Norah Nuttall, Elizabeth Adams and Maureen Ward. Police were convinced that his victim count ran into triple figures (including the victims previously mentioned in this profile) but, as is the case with most prolific killers, they prosecuted him for a few cases which offered the clearest forensic proof.

The evidence against Shipman was overwhelming. His patients had mainly been energetic and in good spirits up until his often-unexpected visit, and morphine had been found in their tissues post-mortem. In other instances, the police had found records that said patients were being prescribed diamorphine by the doctor – yet, when they contacted these patients, they found that they'd never been given the drug and didn't have conditions that warranted its use. It was obvious that Shipman had been stockpiling diamorphine so that he could kill other patients with impunity. Phials of the drug – and morphine tablets – had been found in a carrier bag at his home.

On 25th November, the doctor himself took the stand. He admitted changing his computer records, but said that he had only done so to bring his written accounts in line with information that his patients had given him several months before.

He could give no explanation as to why his patients had ended up with huge amounts of morphine in their systems and also failed to explain why he had never called an ambulance and why he had been so insistent that there was no need for a post-mortem, even when the distraught families said that they wanted one.

On 24th January 2000, the jury retired to consider their verdict, returning a week later with a guilty verdict for all fifteen murders. He was also found guilty of forging Kathleen Grundy's will. Only then was the court told about his previous conviction for forging pethidine prescriptions for his own use.

Mr Justice Forbes described the doctor's acts as 'sheer wickedness' before passing fifteen life sentences plus four years for forging the will. He recommended that Shipman never be released. The doctor, who could hardly have been surprised by the verdict, showed no emotion. Neither did his wife.

Life behind bars

Shipman was initially sent to Strangeways Prison, then moved to Preston, then Walton Jail in Liverpool, before being returned to Strangeways. He lost two stone in weight during his first few weeks of incarceration and aged visibly, but he had the support of Primrose, who visited weekly and would sit, holding his hand and kissing him. His adult children sometimes accompanied her.

In prison, Shipman continued to show two different sides of himself. He helped some prisoners write letters home and helped others to understand their own medical histories, but he was so arrogant when he took part in the prison's quiz team that he was told to leave.

Life was now unspeakably dull for the doctor, so, on 30th April 2001, he agreed to be taken for questioning to Halifax Police Station. There, police asked him about other possible murders he had committed as a GP, but, his natural arrogance reasserting itself, he refused to answer any of their questions, preferring to lean back in his chair, fold his arms and close his eyes. He made it clear that he despised them and their ongoing inquiries. He thought he was totally in control.

The Shipman Inquiry

Both the medical fraternity and the general public had been shocked at the fact that the doctor had apparently murdered with impunity since as early as 1970, and the authorities agreed to set up an inquiry. It began in June 2001 in Manchester and looked into 887 deaths.

Dame Janet Smith, the High Court Judge who chaired the inquiry, concluded that the doctor had killed 215 patients between 1974 and 1998 and that he had possibly killed another 45. In a further 38 cases, there wasn't enough evidence to make a decision.

Suicide

The years passed, and Shipman must have contemplated his life and realised that he had nothing to look forward to. By now, he was resident in Wakefield Prison and was no longer on suicide watch, as the authorities believed he'd come to terms with prison life.

Just before 6 a.m. on 13th January 2004 – the day before his fifty-eighth birthday – he tore a strip from his bed sheet, wound it around his neck and around the bars of his cell window, and hanged himself. As he had died before his sixtieth birthday, his widow got a lump sum of £100,000, plus £18,000 a year from his pension fund.

The motive

So what was the motive for the murders? They weren't acts of mercy as most of the women were happy and reasonably healthy, with strong links to the community, and it wasn't sexual, for one woman surprised Shipman moments after he'd killed her friend and the dead woman's clothing was undisturbed. Interestingly, Shipman was peering into the display cabinet when she walked into the room, and this may tell us something about his motivation. He was like a teenager, left alone to babysit in a stranger's house. Most of us will remember an occasion like this during our teenage years when we peeked into a friend's medicine chest in the bathroom or glanced at a letter on a table-top. It's something that we grow out of as we mature and understand more about a person's right to their own space and privacy.

Shipman, however, may well have become emotionally frozen during his teens at the point when his mother became terminally ill. As such, he would have maintained his level of curiosity about the homes of his patients, derived excitement from rifling through every cupboard and drawer. That said, there wasn't a sadistic element to the doctor's murders – he didn't tell his patients that they were about to die or in any way alarm them – and the drug that he used, diamorphine, gave them a feeling of well-being in the two minutes that it took for them to slip into unconsciousness. Shipman often removed their false teeth at this stage, aware that, as the patient relaxed, their teeth could slip back into their throat and cause a reflex choking. He seemed to want their last minutes to be peaceful, as his mother's had been.

It's clear – given his compulsive need to repeat it – that giving a patient a deadly injection gave him some kind of thrill. He probably had a needle fetish, something that is common in drug users. Even those who have kicked the habit have been known to inject themselves with a saline solution, as they've grown to enjoy the ritual of drug abuse as much as the high. Shipman may have been acting as a sort of 'drug addict by proxy' when he injected his patients, vicariously experiencing their brief, chemically stimulated joy.

Shortly after administering each fatal injection, however, he experienced a level of depression. As such, he was often brusque with the relatives or neighbours of the deceased when they arrived at the scene. It seems that he had to play down the significance of each murder in order to be able to kill again and again.

Another Shipman?

In February 2009, Dame Janet Smith – the judge who investigated Shipman's murders – said that GPs were still signing death certificates for each other, so a 'dishonest, malevolent doctor' could slip through the net. Lessons, apparently, had not been learnt from the most prolific medical killing spree in British history.

In September of that same year, the media revealed that 65 of Shipman's letters, sent to two of his former patients and friends, would be auctioned in November. Written during his years in prison, they were said to be arrogant in tone and repeatedly proclaimed his innocence.

16 Beverly Allitt

Although Beverly originally exhibited Munchausen's syndrome tendencies, where the sufferer harms themselves in order to get attention from friends and medical staff, her behaviour morphed into Munchausen's syndrome by proxy (a diagnosis that some psychologists don't want applied to her case), whereby she harmed other people – with ultimately fatal results.

Early hypochondria

Beverly (later shortened to Bev) Gail Allitt was born on the 4th October 1968 in Corby Glen, a village close to Grantham. Her father, Richard, was a factory worker and her mother, Lillian, had a variety of jobs ranging from seamstress to cleaner. The couple already had a three-year-old daughter when Bev was born and went on to have a third daughter and a son.

Bev enjoyed a holiday with her family every year as well as quite a few day trips. She helped around the house and sometimes brought one or two friends home for tea. She wasn't particularly good at anything, being neither sporty nor academic, but was well liked by her peers.

By her first year at secondary school, she kept complaining of minor illnesses and accidental injuries. One day she'd claim to have stomach cramps, the next day it would be backache. Or she'd breathlessly leave the kitchen holding a bleeding finger, telling her mother that she'd cut it with the bread knife whilst making a sandwich; Lillian was forever having to fetch the bandages and surgical tape. Bev made a great deal of her injuries at school – even the headmaster was aware of her numerous accidents and illnesses. As the year went on, her accounts of what had happened became more grandiose, and she'd claim to have fallen off a horse or her bike, or had been hit a glancing blow by a car.

It was perhaps this immaturity that made her well-liked by younger children, and she became a popular babysitter in the village. That said, she didn't respect other people's boundaries and was guilty of going through their private possessions when left alone in the house.

She was also a compulsive liar, telling her first boyfriend, Kevin – whom she met when she was sixteen – that her parents were so cruel that she'd had to leave home for her own protection. In reality, she was happily living with them. She also told Kevin about her lung disease, kidney problems and grumbling appendix. It was hardly a Romeo and Juliet scenario, so, within a few months, he moved on to a healthier and happier girlfriend.

Bev left school at sixteen and started a pre-nursing course at Grantham College. Sometimes she turned up on crutches, claiming to have hurt her foot, whilst, on other occasions, she had her arm in a sling. Once, she genuinely broke her wrist by falling down the stairs but she told everyone she met that she'd sustained the injury whilst protecting a friend from a girl gang.

The course lasted a year, after which Bev did even more babysitting. She also found herself another boyfriend, a road repairman, and they soon got engaged. He found that she didn't like to be kissed and cuddled and wasn't very keen on sex.

He was amazed at how accident-prone she was, and at how often she ended up at Grantham Hospital's casualty department. By September 1988 she had started her nurse's training there.

She moved into the nursing home and, shortly afterwards, some of the nurses found that their possessions were missing and that a prankster kept hitting the Crash Call button when there wasn't really a medical emergency. But no one initially suspected twenty-year-old Bev, who would bring some of the nurses back to her parents' house to enjoy a home-cooked meal.

Unfortunately her fiancé saw little of her largesse. It was a case of familiarity breeding contempt and she began to cancel dates, and when she did show up, she endlessly found fault with him. In time, the verbal insults were accompanied by physical blows and the relationship came to an end.

As Bev moved into her second year as a trainee nurse, odd things continued to happen at the nursing home. Someone smeared faeces on a door and put newspaper-wrapped faeces under a grill, almost setting the kitchen on fire. They also superglued a door lock and superglued a car door. The hospital manager found that four girls, including Bev Allitt, were always in the vicinity when these upsetting incidents occurred and he warned them all that it had to stop. One nurse blamed Bev but she had no proof. The bizarre behaviour ceased after the manager's warning, and, the following spring, Bev moved in with a friend.

Further traits of Munchausen's syndrome

With her fabricated accidents and invented illnesses, Bev had been showing Munchausen's syndrome traits since her mid-teens, but these escalated markedly in her second year of nurse's training. She was looking after other people but perhaps really wanted someone to look after her. In 1990, she made fifty visits to her GP and to casualty, claiming that she had kidney problems, appendicitis and abdominal pain. She also presented herself so repeatedly at casualty with supposed bladder problems that they gave her a catheter, thinking that the discomfort this caused would stop her making false complaints for a while. But Bev loved it as it convinced some of her acquaintances that she was genuinely ill.

Between supposed bouts of illness, the trainee nurse would arrive at casualty with a cut hand, a bruised foot or a bleeding arm – injuries that doctors suspected were self-inflicted. She even managed to persuade a surgeon to remove her supposedly inflamed appendix, but the organ was in perfect condition. A week later, she returned to casualty with the surgical wound bleeding; doctors believed that she had been deliberately pulling at her stitches.

The jobseeker

But, despite always claiming to have one foot in the grave, Bev passed her exams and, in early December 1990, went for her first interview. It was at Grantham Hospital, but they were dismayed at her poor attendance record and scruffy appearance and turned her down. She had missed so much of her nurse's training due to ill health that, though she'd passed her written work, she hadn't put in a sufficient number of hours on the wards. Now she was allowed to make up the time by working on Ward Four, the children's ward.

As her ten weeks of training neared its end, Bev heard of a three-year course for children's nurses in a nearby town and was given an interview. But, again, she was so vague and lost-looking that they turned her down. She pretended not to care and seemed equally unphased when her flatmate's kitten was mysteriously found dead, its head caved in. There again, Bev had been jealous of her flatmate's love for the little creature and now enjoyed having the other woman to herself...

Meanwhile, Ward Four had failed to find the two experienced registered children's nurses they were trying to recruit and remained desperately short staffed. Reluctantly they gave newly qualified state enrolled nurse Bev the job, albeit on a six-month contract. She was mothered by some of the older nurses when she told them that she'd been beaten and harassed by her ex-boyfriend, but these same conscientious nurses would have been alarmed to know that Bev was working at a care home in the evenings – additional work that her contract forbade – as she was saving up to buy a car. Such a lack of rest and relaxation would play havoc with a nurse's energy levels and alertness and could cause her to make mistakes. They'd have been even more shocked if they could have seen into Bev's mind and realised that she was willing to hurt and even kill patients in order to create drama and become one of the medics who sometimes brought them back to life.

On 14th February 1991, Bev told her supervisor that the key to the fridge where the insulin was stored had disappeared. Now someone could help themselves to insulin without there being a record kept…

Liam's murder

In the same week in February 1991 that Bev started work on Ward Four, seven-month-old Liam Taylor was admitted, his bad cold having turned into a chest infection. Bev was his nurse. He stabilised and his parents, Joanne and Chris, went home for a meal and a change of clothes. When they returned,

Liam's condition had deteriorated markedly and he was immobile and unnaturally pale. Nurse Allitt said that the child had vomited and defecated all over her, that he would probably have died if he'd been at home. Later, Liam's father asked Bev if the little boy would be better off at the nearby Nottingham hospital, Queen's Medical Centre, which had recently opened an intensive care unit for children, but Bev lied that the other hospital was too busy to give their son special care.

Liam's colour soon returned and he began kicking his little legs and smiling at his parents, so the medical team were shocked when he went into cardiac arrest. Bev screamed for the crash cart and the team resuscitated him, but two days later, on 21st February, he had another baffling arrest and stopped breathing for fifteen minutes, resulting in massive brain damage. His devastated parents held him until he died.

Some of the nurses were in tears but, for Bev, it was business as usual. Though some found her cold, others were impressed at her stoicism.

Autopsy

The hospital had thought that Liam had pneumonia and possibly septicaemia, but an autopsy showed that the left ventricle of his heart was so badly damaged as to be almost completely destroyed. In short, he'd apparently had a heart attack, which is very rare in babies. Dr Nanayakkara was unconvinced and requested a second post-mortem, but by then the death certificate had been issued so the baby was duly cremated. Liam's father, Chris, spoke to various doctors and experts in an attempt to find out how such a tiny child could die of cardiac arrest, but they just muttered that they didn't know.

Tim's murder

Two weeks later, eleven-year-old Tim Hardwick was brought into Grantham having had an epileptic fit. He had cerebral palsy, was almost blind, had never learnt to speak, had little motor control and weighed only two-and-a-half stone. By the time he was admitted to Grantham he had stabilised and was soon sleeping peacefully. Then Bev attended to him and suddenly he became a medical emergency and she called for the crash team, saying that he had gone into cardiac arrest. Despite doctors' attempts to resuscitate him, he was declared dead within half an hour of Nurse Allitt sounding the alarm.

The autopsy showed some small bleeds into Tim's lungs, more usually associated with asphyxia, but the epileptic fits could have caused such bleeding, so the doctor put epilepsy as the cause of death, even though Tim hadn't had a fit in the four to five hours before his death.

Kayley's close call

Three days later, one-year-old Kayley Desmond was admitted to the ward suffering from a chest infection. She seemed stable, but suddenly Bev called another nurse into the room and pointed out that the child had gone a strange colour. Bev phoned for the crash team while the other nurse resuscitated the baby, whose heart had stopped. Once they had resuscitated her, medics did tests on the now-screaming child but could find nothing wrong.

At four that morning, her heart stopped again for no clear reason. Medics got it started and transferred her to the intensive care unit of the Queen's Medical Centre. Bev volunteered to go with her in the ambulance.

By now, the senior nurses at Grantham Hospital were baffled. Most had a decade or two's worth of experience and had seen only one or two cardiac arrests in children. Yet, suddenly, there had been three in a few days.

Paul's lucky escape

A five-month-old boy called Paul Crampton was the next to suffer unexplained and potentially fatal symptoms. He was admitted to Ward Four on 20th March suffering from a bronchial infection but had improved significantly and was due to go home the following day. To everyone's consternation, he suddenly went grey and Bev told one of her colleagues that he was 'having a hypo'. She did a test for hypoglycaemia but the result was low-normal and the other nurses were relieved. But, a few minutes later, the baby went limp and sweaty so they did another test, which now confirmed Bev's original diagnosis. The team hooked the baby up to a dextrose drip and he recovered within twenty minutes – but without their prompt treatment he would have slipped into a coma with potentially fatal results.

The following day, Paul went grey and unresponsive again, his eyes rolling back in his head. Doctors reattached him to the drip but he remained seriously unwell. It would later be alleged that Nurse Allitt gave him three separate overdoses of insulin that day. Concerned staff transferred him to the Queen's Medical Centre – accompanied by Bev and the paramedics – and he lived. But, back home, he cried a lot as though reliving a frightening ordeal.

Bradley's torment

The following day, Bev called another nurse and pointed out that five-year-old Bradley Gibson, recovering from pneumonia, had suddenly lost consciousness. Medics found that he had high levels of potassium in his bloodstream, but that didn't explain why he had gone into cardiac arrest. Indeed, his symptoms were so odd that the doctors wondered if he'd mistakenly been given the wrong drug. A nurse gave him mouth to mouth resuscitation, after which – still in a coma – he was swiftly transferred to the Nottingham intensive care unit, where he regained consciousness but was a very ill boy. He crawled now rather than walked and cried because his legs hurt so much.

Bradley refused to speak to the nurses, and would turn his head to the wall if one approached him, whereas before he had been a talkative and happy child. Fortunately, he began to get his mobility back and was discharged, though he had terrible nightmares and drew pictures of himself in bed with someone looming menacingly above.

Yik's terror

A few days later, on 28th March, two-year-old Yik Hung Chan was admitted with a fractured skull after falling from his first floor bedroom. He made a speedy recovery and, by the end of the month, was racing around the ward. So everyone was surprised when Bev told one of her Chinese colleagues that he was crying and asked her to speak to him in his native tongue. The nurse hurried to the little boy, only to find that he'd turned blue. Bev helped the other nurses to administer oxygen, and the child revived. At her happiest in the midst of a crisis, Bev travelled with him in the ambulance to the Queen's Medical Centre, where he made a full recovery.

Becky's death

Allitt's next patient, two-month-old Becky Phillips, wasn't so fortunate. The baby girl, who had been born three months prematurely, was admitted to Ward Four because she was vomiting up her feed. She stabilised, so a nurse was surprised when Bev said that the baby had gone cold and clammy. To the more experienced medic, the child seemed fine. Bev voiced her concerns again the following day as nurses prepared to discharge the baby, but again she was overruled.

Becky's overjoyed parents took her home and reunited her with her twin, Katie. But, by the evening, Becky's eyes were rolling about and she screamed as if in pain. The couple called the doctor out but he said it was probably just a touch of colic; by now, the little girl appeared to be more peaceful. When the family woke the following morning, however, they found that Becky had stopped breathing. They raced her to Grantham Hospital's casualty department where she was pronounced dead. Staff attributed the fatality to sudden infant death syndrome (SIDS), more commonly known as cot death. In other words, she had died of unknown causes.

The subsequent autopsy would show that her heart had blistered, unusual for such a young baby, but the cause of death remained SIDS. Ironically, Bev was so nice to Becky's parents, Sue and Peter Phillips, that they made her godmother to Katie, their surviving twin.

Katie's paralysis

As a precaution, the hospital admitted Katie and hooked her up to an apnoea monitor to keep a check on her breathing. She was perfectly fine and eventually her parents went home to start planning for her sister's funeral, leaving Katie in Nurse Allitt's supposedly capable hands.

Shortly afterwards, Bev alerted the other nurses that Katie had turned blue. They revived her and kept watch by her bedside. The night sister, Jean Savill, started her shift early and stayed with the baby, refusing Bev's repeated offers to give her a break. The following day, her parents took turns by her bedside, even sleeping there overnight.

By the next morning, when Katie hadn't had a repeated attack, everyone relaxed, convinced that the crisis was over, and Katie was left alone for a couple of minutes. Medics heard the baby crying, then Bev came racing out of the ward holding her – to everyone's alarm, the infant was bright red and breathless. Despite their best efforts, the crash team thought that she had died, then her heart restarted. However, she went into convulsions and the worried medics transferred her to the Queen's Medical Centre, where she was immediately hooked up to a life support machine.

It was found that the nine-week-old had suffered permanent brain damage due to oxygen deprivation, damage that left her partially paralysed and partially blind. Much later, when her X-rays were examined, they would show that someone had squeezed her so hard that her bones had fractured and her ribs had broken.

A mysterious virus

By now, the staff at Grantham Hospital, particularly those associated with Ward Four, knew that there was something very wrong on the ward but there were so many variables that it was hard to pinpoint what was happening. Was there an infection in the hospital or were the babies being admitted already suffering from some unrecognised virus? Had they been given a bad batch of drugs or was something wrong with the food or the water supply? The night sister, Jean Savill, asked for extra staff and for swabs and tests but, due to funding cutbacks, her requests remained unfulfilled.

Jean Savill then wrote to her superiors, pointing out that there had been an unprecedented seven cardiac arrests in the past three months. She again asked for additional staff and was given temporary access to a couple of nurses from the adult wards. She also asked for a defibrillator to be based in the ward – they were using the one based in casualty – but, as this cost £6,000, she had to settle for a few child-sized paddles instead. Jean Savill was a hero in all of this, making herself unpopular with management in order to get the best care for her patients.

Michael's cardiac arrest

The patients' suffering continued. Six-year-old Michael Davidson was admitted on 7th April suffering from an accidental airgun wound that had caused a little bleeding. Surgeons removed the pellet from his chest and, two days later, he was recovering well, sitting up and playing games. Bev Allitt prepared a dose of what should have been antibiotics and handed it to another nurse to give to him – but the syringe actually contained a potassium overdose, causing the child to suddenly arch his back, go rigid, turn blue and have a cardiac arrest. Fortunately, he had made a spontaneous recovery by the time the crash team arrived.

A second autopsy

By now, one of the head doctors was sufficiently alarmed that he asked the Phillipses to delay the funeral of nine-week-old Becky in order that the pathologist could do a second post-mortem. Meanwhile, tests at the pathology lab had shown that Paul Crampton's blood, taken during his seizures at Grantham Hospital, contained more than 30 times the normal level of insulin, but another doctor decided that the lab had made a mistake and the police were not called.

Two further attacks

The next child to suffer a cardiac arrest was eight-week-old Chris Peasgood, admitted with a chest infection. Bev told his mother to go outside and have a smoke – and, when she came back, the child was fighting for his life.

The medics revived him and his nurse, Clare Winser, took up a vigil by his bed. Bev Allitt offered to take over to let Clare go to the ladies' room and, when she returned, the baby was so close to death that a priest was called in to perform a baptism.

Clare begged his mother to ask for him to be transferred to the Queen's Medical Centre, warning her that he would be dead before morning if he stayed on Ward Four. Despite the fact that he wasn't her patient, Bev insisted on accompanying him in the ambulance.

That same month, another Christopher – with the surname of King – was also fighting for his life. He had been recovering well from his operation but deteriorated markedly after Bev Allitt fed him, giving him milk when he was on a post-operative diet of water. Something added to the milk caused him to have a heart attack but he was transferred to Nottingham's intensive care unit and survived.

A growing awareness

In the same time frame, one of Grantham Hospital's doctors attended a symposium about Munchausen's syndrome by proxy. The lecturer, top paediatrician David Southall, explained that, if a series of unexpected respiratory arrests occurred and were always in the presence of one person, the doctors should consider MBP and install surveillance cameras. He added that doctors in Chelsea had done so over a five-year period and had observed fourteen MBP mothers secretly suffocating their children. During this time, Grantham's night sister, Jean Savill, wrote to the management noting that Bev Allitt had been present at more than 20 cardiac arrests in the last two months.

Other nurses began to kid Bev that she must be carrying some mysterious virus that she was passing on to the children. Bev laughed and seemed to enjoy being the centre of attention, but one or two of the nurses also noticed that she enjoyed the excitement of a cardiac arrest, was always at the very core of the action when they were reviving a child and insisted on being the one to escort the child to the Queen's Medical Centre in the ambulance.

Patrick's convulsions

The following day – 18th April – seven-week-old Patrick Elstone was admitted to the ward suffering from gastro-enteritis. That afternoon, Bev alerted the other nurses that he looked ill and, when they checked, they found that he was barely breathing. Fortunately, he revived in the treatment room, but a few hours later, Bev again raised the alarm to say that he was blue and breathless. Someone had mysteriously disconnected his apnoea monitor, which would have given off a telltale shriek the moment his breathing stopped.

The crash team revived him and he was transferred to the Queen's Medical Centre. A doctor from Grantham, suspecting that the child had met with foul play, phoned the Centre and asked them to check his insulin levels. Some of the senior staff had a meeting to voice their concerns but still no one phoned the police and this left the killer free to strike for a final time.

Claire's death

On 22nd April, fifteen-month-old Claire Peck's parents brought her into Grantham as she had suffered a serious asthma attack. Left alone with Bev for a few minutes, she turned blue, went rigid and stopped breathing. A doctor stabilised her and went into the corridor to speak to her parents, telling them that they were going to transfer her to Nottingham, but Bev appeared at his side, shrieking, 'She's gone blue again' and, this time, despite Herculean efforts from the hospital's medics, the baby died.

Tests taken half an hour after she expired showed that her potassium levels were off the scale, but, as potassium leaks from the red blood cells several hours after death, the pathologist decided that she had died of natural causes – specifically, an asthma attack.

Four days later, an empty cot in Ward Four was found ablaze and the hospital fire officer found that it was deliberate. Shortly afterwards, doctors phoned the police. They told detectives about the suspiciously high number of deaths and near-fatal episodes in the past two months, about their fears that a Munchausen's syndrome by proxy killer was stalking the ward.

Missing evidence

That April, at Grantham Hospital, someone stole the allocation book, without which it was difficult to ascertain which nurses had been responsible for which children. One of the senior nursing staff had written the shifts in her work diary but found that the relevant pages had been torn out.

Fortunately, determined police reassembled the information by careful questioning of nurses and the children's relatives, ascertaining that only Nurse Allitt had been in attendance during all twenty cardiac arrests.

Questioned

On Tuesday 21st May 1991, police woke Bev Allitt up at 7 a.m. and arrested her for stealing the key to the insulin safe and for the attempted murder of Paul Crampton. Though they repeatedly questioned her at the station for the next 24 hours, she denied everything. Out on bail, she told everyone that she was innocent, that the police didn't know what they were talking about.

The detectives continued their inquiries, finding samples of some of the children's blood and tissues. Often the X-rays and samples had mysteriously gone missing, but they collected several that showed foul play. Paul Crampton had astronomically high levels of insulin in his blood and Liam Taylor's heart had stopped because he'd been asphyxiated or poisoned. Becky Phillips had also been murdered, as a huge dose of insulin had been injected into her bloodstream.

Further MBP behaviour

Three weeks after her release from custody, Bev took her god-daughter, little Katie Phillips, out in her pram despite the little girl's mother, Sue, protesting that it was raining. Sue had heard about Bev's arrest but believed that it must be a case of mistaken identity as Bev had been so nice to them. The couple even offered to help pay her lawyers' fees.

A few minutes later Bev returned, shrieking, 'Call the doctor – she's about to have a convulsion.' The child seemed fine but, having already lost Katie's twin, Sue was taking no chances. As she dialled her GP, she saw her daughter break out into a heavy sweat then start to moan.

Bev left and the child was admitted to Ward Four, where she continued to have strange choking fits and loss of appetite. When detectives heard that the illness had only come on after she was left alone with Bev Allitt, they seized all medications in the Phillipses' house in case she had tampered with them.

Suspended from duty, Bev was perpetually bored. A motherly woman called Eileen Jobson – who lived with her teenage son Jonathan – took her in, but soon found that money was going missing from her purse and that, later, the purse itself disappeared. Someone left the plug in the sink with the water turned on and someone scorched an area of carpet with a cigarette lighter. Bev tried to blame all of this on poltergeist activity and said that she often saw ghosts.

Bev shouted for them one day and showed them a knife that was stuck deep into Jonathan's pillow. She said that a poltergeist must have done it. The teenager was so afraid that they all moved into his grandmother's house for the night. There, Bev allegedly discovered a knife stuck into the pillow she was about to use.

Dangerous

Police continued to amass evidence against the deadly nurse. They found that Liam Taylor, Tim Hardwick, Bradley Gibson and Claire Peck had probably been poisoned with potassium chloride, as their blood showed unnaturally high levels and such an overdose perfectly explained their symptoms. And only Bev had been in attendance at all 23 cardiac arrests.

Meanwhile, Eileen Jobson's son, Jonathan, became ill with shooting pains in his legs, though he got better when Bev was admitted to hospital suffering from what appeared to be a breast infection. Doctors found that she was faking her symptoms by heating up the thermometer and injecting water into her own breast.

They sent her back to Eileen's and she gave Jonathan a glass of juice. Shortly afterwards his vision faded, he went grey and clammy and lost consciousness, but Jonathan revived quickly and doctors believed that he'd fainted due to the hot sun.

Bev also continued to self-harm, breaking her catheter on two occasions so that part of it remained inside her bladder and had to be removed at the hospital. She was readmitted after describing symptoms that suggested she had a brain tumour, but a scan showed no abnormalities and doctors realised that there was nothing wrong with her.

Bev's malice continued to wreak havoc, even though she was no longer working on Ward Four. The night sister, Jean Savill, was so upset to hear about the murders that she took a paracetamol overdose and was found dead at the home she shared with her husband, and some of the bereaved parents found that their marriages were breaking down due to depression and stress.

The former nurse also gave tablets to her landlady's dog and it collapsed, foaming at the mouth, but survived after coughing up two tablets. On another occasion, her landlady saw Bev tormenting a cat.

A murder charge

On Tuesday, 3rd September, police arrested Bev Allitt and charged her with Becky Phillips's murder. She remained cool under questioning and, after eight hours, they let her go. Later that month, she hit her flatmate during a row and the other girl left, went to the police and told them about the violence. Detectives also found out about a suspicious death at the care home where Bev had worked.

On 20th November they rearrested her and charged her with murdering four children, attempting to murder nine children and causing grievous bodily harm to the latter. She refused to answer their questions and soon went to sleep in her cell.

Anorexic

In New Hall Women's Prison in Wakefield, awaiting trial, Bev regularly arrived at the prison doctor's with what appeared to be self-inflicted minor injuries. When these failed to get her the attention she needed, she told the authorities that she could no longer face food. In early January 1992 she claimed to have stopped eating and, by June, she had lost four stone. After this, she began to vomit in front of the prison officers, who were understandably baffled – if she wasn't eating, how could she be vomiting? Concerned, they transferred her to the local hospital, posting a guard outside her door.

There, doctors discovered that she was swallowing her own faeces – though, as she still wasn't eating, they were surprised that she could produce so much excrement. She was moved to Rampton, the high security hospital for mentally ill prisoners, where she continued to self-harm.

Trial

Her trial began at Nottingham on 15th February 1993. The prosecution had wanted to tell the jury about a possible motive, Munchausen's syndrome by proxy. They could produce two psychiatric reports testifying that Bev was suffering from this, but the judge ruled that these would suggest that Bev was crazy and might encourage the jury to convict her regardless of the other evidence.

There was no shortage of witnesses at the trial, as nurses and bereaved parents took the stand, each testifying to the fact that Bev had always been present when the children developed life-threatening symptoms and illnesses.

Back in her room at Rampton one night, Bev collapsed through lack of food and was taken to the nearest hospital, where she was fed via a tube.

The court case continued without her, the prosecution producing witnesses for eleven weeks. In contrast, the defence could only fill three days with paid-for testimony from scientists.

On 11th May, the jury retired. Twelve days later, on the 23rd, they returned and, over the next four days, declared her guilty of murdering Liam Taylor, Tim Hardwick, Becky Phillips and Claire Peck. She was also found guilty of nine counts of grievous bodily harm.

When she was told about the outcome of the trial by her lawyer, Bev Allitt wept briefly in her hospital bed, then demanded that doctors remove the tube that was keeping her alive. She said that she wanted to die, but soon began to eat again. She was subsequently sentenced to thirteen concurrent life sentences, with the judge recommending that she serve a minimum of 40 years.

An inquiry into the deaths led to the Treasury providing £500,000 to give compensation to the parents of children who were killed or injured.

A bid for freedom

Bev Allitt is still serving her life sentence at Rampton, which, being a hospital, is less austere than a prison. Several years ago, she appeared briefly in a televised documentary, looking slightly stocky but healthy. She answered the reporter's questions about her daily routine but left the room as soon as she was asked about her crimes. She had previously announced that she had become engaged to a male patient at the hospital and hoped to marry him.

In 2006, Allitt caused controversy when she launched an appeal for a reduced sentence. Crime writers pointed out that, if she were released, she would be young enough to have children and could essentially grow her own victims. Also, one of her surviving patients, Michael Davidson, gave an interview to a women's magazine about his ordeal and said that life should definitely mean life.

In December 2007, the High Court ruled that she would have to serve at least 30 years in prison, so she will be 54 (and statistically post-menopausal) before she can apply for parole.

A psychological assessment

Intrigued by the many different opinions held by both crime writers and the public about Allitt's mental health and motivation, I contacted forensic psychologist Dr David A Holmes, author of *Abnormal, Clinical and Forensic Psychology* and

The Essence of Abnormal Psychology. Dr Holmes, whose specialist areas include Munchausen's syndrome by proxy, also featured in an ITV documentary about Beverly Allitt and her crimes. The interview took place in September 2009 and Dr Holmes's replies are italicised.

CAD: Beverly Allitt's childhood, as far as we know, was unexceptional, yet she became a remorseless killer. Was she born with a personality disorder? What, in your opinion, informed her callous acts?

Dr H: *I think she was born with a personality distortion – this usually entails the development of more than one disorder from formative traits in childhood. She clearly had the ability to lie almost pathologically, easily convincing others of various stories that gained her attention. This is a warning sign of fledgling psychopathy. She also set fires and was reported to have killed a flatmate's pet, which are two of the predictive signs of a serial killer. Psychopaths, sadists and killers often report harsh, inconsistent punishment in childhood. This may brutalise and teach violence as a means to an end. However, it is equally as often a reaction to the antisocial, uncaring and provocative behaviour of the developing deviant by parents, who will share the same unempathic, reactive genetic traits. In Allitt's case, her feigning illness probably acted to avert punishment or harsh treatment as she would retreat into her 'sick' role. She was also poor academically and barely qualified to nurse but compensated by being very focused on patients and manipulating relatives, which is another sign of how psychopaths may 'charm and disarm' others.*

Allitt's repeatedly feigned illness from an early age is a sign of factitious or Munchausen's disorder, which is often a precursor to, and accompanies, MBP. This continued throughout her development and adulthood. Allitt had 100 days off during her nursing training, probably feigned illness.

CAD: I've always believed her to be a classic case of Munchausen's syndrome by proxy but some true crime writers reject this classification for her. Any thoughts?

Dr H: *Allitt had all the signs of MBP with Munchausen's syndrome from childhood: pathological lying, psychopathic lack of empathy or consequences for others. Even when caught and held she still feigned illness, portrayed herself as a victim and showed no remorse or feelings as she distanced herself from the acts whilst focusing on her own plight. She competed with doctors and portrayed herself as an emergency angel of mercy rather than the Pied Piper of childcare.*

MBP is not a popular disorder and a substantial movement exists in most countries who deny a mother or female carer could hurt children, despite unambiguous video footage of them doing just that. Those who report cases are often attacked publicly and privately. This becomes more of an issue with a nurse employed in the health system. Allitt's case had to be vetted by the Home Secretary because of the political implications of a health service employing potential killers (such as her and Colin Norris). She was the first UK nurse to face child-harm charges.

CAD: At Rampton, she starved herself and also ingested faeces. Do you see this as a form of self-hatred or was it an attempt to prove to the public that she was mad, therefore ensuring that she wouldn't be moved from a hospital environment?

Dr H: *These acts of starvation and eating faeces are extensions of her Munchausen behaviour and manipulation of the situation she was in. This serves the purpose of getting her attention, sympathy and special privileges. It also helped her towards pleading insanity as mitigation, and feigning insanity placed her in the relative comfort of a special hospital not prison. She was clearly forensically aware of such issues in the fearless, dispassionate way she reacted to arrest and simply slept in the holding cell without agitation or concern.*

CAD: Do you view her as mad, bad, sad or a combination of these?

Dr H: *I think she is personality-disordered and this lies between mad and bad. Her 'condition', having psychopathic and MBP traits should not reduce the 'bad' or punishment aspect of her crimes but should only be an issue in the length of sentence, which should be indefinite until she poses no risk. Her traits are aggravating, not mitigating. The fact she has no empathy simply makes her dangerous, not mad or sad.*

17   Charles Cullen

If this nurse's confession is true, he got away with killing patients for a remarkably long period, spanning from 1988 to 2003. Unusually, he admitted his crimes to detectives in detail, giving information which subsequently appeared in numerous newspaper and magazine features, television documentaries and books.

An impoverished childhood

Charles was born on the 22nd February 1960 to Florence and Edmond Cullen in New Jersey. They were staunch Catholics and he was their eighth child.

The family were already poor but their finances took a turn for the worst when Edmond, a bus driver, died that summer. His widow still had seven children living at home and she struggled to cope. Charles was bullied for wearing hand-me-down clothes and was so unhappy that, at nine, he swallowed the chemicals from a chemistry set in the hope of committing suicide. It spoke of his level of desperation, as children of this age group rarely try to kill themselves. When he was seventeen, his mother died in a car crash, leaving him orphaned. Charles had been her youngest child and they were very close.

Devastated, Charles dropped out of school and, in April 1978, enlisted in the navy. After a year's training he was assigned to work on a submarine but was so thin and pale that he was bullied mercilessly by the other sailors. Too timid to defend himself, he often took refuge in the ship's sick bay, where he became friends with the naval doctor and admitted that he liked helping people and that he wanted to become a nurse. One day he took his fantasy too far, sneaking into the medical bay and dressing in the doctor's green scrubs, mask and gloves. He was formally disciplined for this.

Charles was discharged from the navy on 30th March 1984 – rumours would later circulate that he'd made another suicide attempt and had been let go because of psychiatric problems, but the navy refused to comment on this. Returning to his home town in New Jersey, he registered as a student at nursing school.

The new nurse

Charles applied himself rigorously to his studies, achieved mostly As and Bs, and graduated after three years with a nursing degree. Two months before he graduated, one of his brothers committed suicide.

In May 1987, Charles became a registered nurse and, the following month, he married his girlfriend, Adrienne, who worked in a computer lab. He secured a job at St Barnabas Medical Center in Livingston, New Jersey, working in the burns unit. His colleagues found that he was a man of few words and that he lacked the easy manner of most of the female nurses, but he was efficient and always accepted overtime.

Murder

In the summer of 1988, a 72-year-old patient, John Yengo, was admitted to the unit suffering from a severe allergic skin reaction. Two weeks after his admittance, Charles Cullen injected his intravenous tube with a fatal dose of the heart drug lidocaine. Afterwards, he portrayed himself as the hero who had battled tirelessly – albeit fruitlessly – to restart the patient's heart.

Shortly afterwards he became employed by a different health service and, though he still worked at St Barnabas, he was no longer permanently attached to the burns unit. Instead, he spent time in whichever department needed him – everything from cardiac to intensive care.

Whenever possible, Charles elected to work the graveyard shift, beloved of nurses who are serial killers. With no visitors and few medics around, he was free to do as he wanted, and that suited the secretive nurse just fine.

His first daughter was born that year but he proved to be a remote father, preferring to be at work or slumped in front of the television, drinking heavily. The couple had a second daughter in 1992, after which the marriage deteriorated further; by now, Charles rarely spoke to his wife. He had wild mood swings, was often angry and so antisocial that he would barely say hello to their neighbours. Adrienne became increasingly afraid of him and began to consider divorce.

Dangerous behaviour

Charles's spouse wasn't the only person who had had enough of him – the administrators at St

Barnabas had begun to suspect that someone was tampering with the patients IV bags. They believed that Charles had contaminated one of these bags of fluid with insulin and responded by refusing to give him any further shifts. However, they didn't make their findings official and Charles moved on to a new nursing post at Warren Hospital, also in New Jersey, this time working in the coronary care unit.

During this time, Adrienne reported her husband twice for domestic violence and, in January 1993, she filed for divorce, citing his extreme cruelty – he had beaten and even killed several of their family pets and would do bizarre things such as refusing to let her heat the house in winter. Now, Charles feared being alone, so again attempted suicide and spent several days in a psychiatric facility.

Further deaths

Charles's heavy drinking had descended into alcoholism and the courts would only give him limited access to his two daughters for fear that he would harm them. He was prescribed antidepressants but sometimes neglected to take them, whereupon his already morose mood would darken further. It's possible that he committed most of his murders during this 'down' time, creating excitement in an otherwise dull and flat day or night.

Charles slipped into ninety-year-old Lucy Mugavero's room on 9th March 1993 and injected her IV bag with an overdose of digoxin, a heart stimulant. She was only in hospital for a minor lung problem and was from a family who lived long lives – one of her brothers would reach the age of a hundred. But ninety is still considered to be a ripe old age so there was no autopsy.

Charles also continued to cause havoc in his private life, virtually stalking a nurse who refused to go out with him. He even broke into her home and moved some of her belongings around. She contacted the police, who put a tap on her phone and Charles was trapped when he phoned her the following day and confessed to the incident. He was arrested and charged and told he'd be given a court date in due course. The following day he again attempted suicide.

In April, his estranged wife, Adrienne, filed a restraining order against him, which was later granted. Charles spent some time in a psychiatric facility before returning to work.

In June, he represented himself in court, trying to get access to his children, and in July, he used digoxin to kill one of his patients, 85-year-old Mary Natoli; when Charles's life was in chaos, he got his revenge on society by killing its most vulnerable citizens.

In August, the nurse pleaded guilty to breaking into his colleague's home. Afterwards, he tried to take his own life for the umpteenth time, but he was always ambivalent as, though he hated his current situation and wanted to end it, he was afraid of death.

Accused of murder

In the autumn of 1993, Charles was accused of murder by the son of a deceased patient, Helen Dean. She had been operated on for cancer and had recovered so was about to be moved to a nursing home, but Charles came in and gave her an injection, after which her condition deteriorated. She complained to her son about the nurse who had stuck a needle in her leg and he took his concerns to her oncologist, who confirmed that she wasn't due for an injection and that the registered nurse was not empowered to administer them. Helen appeared to have survived the jab but died later that day. At her son's insistence, the hospital conducted an internal inquiry and Helen Dean was autopsied, but they didn't test for digoxin and the autopsy was inconclusive.

Charles was given a lie detector test by police but this, too, was inconclusive and no charges were filed; he continued to work at the hospital. However, his increasingly suspicious colleagues cold-shouldered him and, on 1st December, he resigned.

The death toll mounts

The following April, Charles started work at Hunterdon Medical Center, New Jersey in the intensive care unit.

In June 1994, he received a nursing licence to work in Pennsylvania and, at the end of that year, his acrimonious divorce was finalised. There followed a couple of years in which he dated a married woman and was working hard to persuade her to leave her husband for him. He also continued his fight through the court system to have overnight access visits with his daughters.

By the start of 1996, however, the affair was going downhill and Charles resumed his killing spree. On 21st January, he gave 71-year-old Leroy Sinn a fatal dose of digoxin. The father of four had been active up until his admission to hospital, working full-time and also taking on the role of elder in his local church.

On 31st May, Earl Young also died of a digoxin overdose. The 75-year-old navy veteran had been enjoying his time in a retirement home and wasn't expected to die in hospital. Nine days later, Charles gave 49-year-old Catherine Dext an unprescribed injection of the heart drug. The respected prison officer promptly expired.

Twenty-four days later, the nurse murdered 65-year-old former teacher Frank Mazzacco. Again, Charles's trademark digoxin was responsible.

On 10th July, eighty-year-old Jesse Eichlin collapsed at his local church, was given CPR by a fellow churchgoer and taken to hospital. Shortly after being attended to by the serial-killing nurse, he died.

It was apparent that Charles enjoyed the part of hospital life that most medics hate, namely witnessing the grief of the dead person's relatives. Charles Cullen rarely approached the bereaved directly, but he hung around outside the door of many of the death rooms or pretended to nurse other patients who were in the next bed to someone who had just died. Lonely and embittered, he was in constant emotional pain and seemed to enjoy witnessing others in similar distress.

In October, his girlfriend ended their liaison and Charles resigned from the hospital where they worked together, then had second thoughts and asked for his job back. Perhaps tellingly, they refused to reinstate him and he began to look for other work.

The following month, Charles started a new nursing job at Morrisontown Memorial Hospital but he was soon being written up for various infringements, including ignoring a doctor's order to stop giving sedatives to a patient. More alarmingly, he was seen to tamper with the oxygen setting on a ventilator. On another occasion, he was supposed to give an anti-coagulant drug to a patient but failed to do so, putting them at risk of a thrombosis clot. In August 1997, the hospital had had enough and fired him for poor performance.

Unemployed, Charles spent hours tending his garden, attacking any cat that happened to stray over his seed beds. He bought himself a dog for company but the poor animal was removed by animal welfare officers after neighbours reported that he was ill-treating it. In early autumn, he was again treated for clinical depression as an inpatient at a psychiatric facility.

By 1998, the out-of-work nurse had run up large heating and accommodation bills and filed for bankruptcy, but his finances – and his spirits – improved when he landed a job at the Liberty Nursing and Rehabilitation Center in Allentown, Pennsylvania. Charles hadn't worked in a nursing home before and was eager to be left alone with the mainly elderly residents. The building had a ventilator unit that helped seriously ill patients with their breathing and he was posted there. On 7th May, an elderly man who was recovering from injuries sustained in a car crash, began to vomit and tests showed abnormally high insulin levels. Medics stabilised him but, several days later, he went into a coma and died on the 19th May. Another nurse was blamed for giving the patient an accidental dose and she was suspended, though she pointed out that Charles, who was treating the dead man's room-mate, was a likely suspect. She also pointed out that Charles was already under suspicion for taking medical supplies that he wasn't authorised to use.

Three months later, nurses found Charles struggling with an elderly woman. He claimed that he was trying to give her an anti-anxiety drug but that she'd resisted him and broken her arm. As he wasn't even her nurse, the hospital fired him.

Another nursing post

A week later Charles began working on the intensive care unit at Easton Hospital in Wilson, Pennsylvania. On paper, he looked good as he had no family, was prepared to work the unpopular graveyard shift and was very keen to do overtime. He also worked part-time at the burns unit in Leigh Valley Hospital, as he was keen to earn enough money to pay off his outstanding bills.

A month after the new nurse started, diabetic Ottomar Schramm was admitted to Easton Hospital's emergency care unit having suffered a seizure. The cancer sufferer was a church elder who enjoyed playing in the church band. Ottomar's relatives saw Charles Cullen in his room with a hypodermic and asked its purpose, and the nurse replied that it would be used if the patient's heart stopped. Three days later, the octogenarian deteriorated rapidly and tests showed that he had a massive dose of digoxin in his system. His relatives were surprised when the thin, pale nurse told them not to ask for an autopsy, though he didn't say why.

But an autopsy *was* performed and administrators were told that the patient shouldn't have had any digoxin in his bloodstream as it hadn't been prescribed for him. Indeed, he had no need of the drug as he had a pacemaker. Toxicology tests were still continuing in March 1999 when Charles quit the job.

Charles now worked exclusively at his other job, in the burns unit at Leigh Valley Hospital. On 31st August 1999, he gave a fatal digoxin overdose to 22-year-old accident victim Matthew

Mattern, later claiming that he'd done so to prevent the young man going through painful surgery.

Another suicide attempt

Whilst killing his patients gave Charles a kind of quiet satisfaction, it wasn't enough to quell his ongoing unhappiness. He disliked himself and his life and saw only loneliness in his future. On 3rd January 2000, in his latest attempt to end it all, he sealed his apartment and inhaled carbon monoxide fumes, having first put his recently acquired pet dog outside. However, a neighbour smelt kerosene, saw that towels were stuffed under the nurse's door and alerted the emergency services. They took a still-conscious Charles to a counselling centre and he was freed to go home the next day. He now spent his non-working hours with one of his brothers, who was terminally ill, and seemed genuinely affected by the man's pain

Once again, however, Charles's colleagues became suspicious of the number of patients who were dying in his care and he left the hospital in April and began to look for another nursing job.

In June, he started work at the critical care unit at St Luke's Hospital in Pennsylvania and, for a while, apparently managed to keep his murderous instincts in check. But by the start of 2001, the urge to take another life had become all-consuming and Charles began to study the patients' records to ascertain who would be easiest to kill.

In February, another of his patients expired unexpectedly. The following month, Charles's brother died of cancer and Charles seemed genuinely sad.

It didn't stop him robbing other people of their relatives, though, and, in June, he gave heart-failure patient 79-year-old Irene Krapf a fatal injection of digoxin. She had been admitted to the ward less than an hour before to have a pacemaker fitted – something that would have given her a new lease of life.

The next patient to receive a potentially fatal overdose was Korean war veteran William Park. The nurse gave him various drugs but, each time, the 72-year-old recovered. On his fourth or fifth murder attempt, Charles returned to his old favourite, digoxin, and, on 8th November 2001, Mr Park died.

Perhaps Charles feared that his colleagues were becoming suspicious because it was December before he killed again, and this time the victim was 72-year-old radio personality Paul Galgon, who'd come in to have a pacemaker fitted. Charles gave him digoxin but Paul survived, whereupon the medic gave him a second dose. Paul died nine hours later. (Eventually Charles would be found guilty of Paul Galgon's attempted murder.)

Later that same winter – in January 2002 – Charles killed eighty-year-old cancer patient Samuel Spangler, who was recovering from a slight heart attack, giving him a drug called nitroprusside, which reduces blood pressure. Samuel's wife of sixty years was amongst the bereaved.

Daniel George, an 82-year-old restaurateur, was the next to suffer a premature death. In May, he was admitted to the ward for a bypass operation, but Charles injected digoxin into his IV tube and Daniel weakened and died. The following month, 72-year-old navy veteran Edward O'Toole met a similar fate, although this time Charles used a paralysing drug, vecoronium.

By now, the staff at St Luke's were alarmed at the death toll, especially on Charles's ward. The number of code blues (emergency resuscitation situations) had doubled since the pallid nurse arrived. When stolen medication was found in the needle bin, there was an investigation and suspicion centred on Charles. He resigned on 7th June 2002.

The administrators of St Luke's reported their concerns over the stolen medication to the Pennsylvania State Nursing Board, but the nurse denied everything and the board took no action against him. One of the nurses, however, figured out that 67 patients had died between January and June 2002, and that 38 of them had died on Charles's shift. She and several of her colleagues made phone calls to various hospital administrators, informing them of their fears.

Undaunted at almost being caught out again, Charles found gainful employment at the Sacred Heart Hospital in Allentown, but a nurse who'd previously worked with him warned staff that people died whenever he was around, so Charles was sacked and moved back to New Jersey, taking a job at the Somerset Medical Center. Meanwhile, various hospital administrators reported their fears to the authorities and detectives began to investigate the troubled nurse.

Addicted to murder

As soon as Charles was familiar with the layout of Somerset Medical Center, he resumed his killing spree. On 12th February 2003, he surreptitiously approached patient Eleanor Stoecker, who had cancer of the kidneys. Though he wasn't her primary nurse, Charles gave her an intravenous injection, whereupon the sixty-year-old's condition deteriorated and she was given the last rites. She died the following morning and the staff explained to her relatives that the cancer plus the chemotherapy had taken a fatal toll.

Eleven days later, Charles killed twice, injecting both 74-year-old Joyce Mangini and 89-year-old Giacomino Toto with a powerful muscle relaxant. The following month, he murdered again, injecting norepinephrine into 83-year-old army veteran John Shanagher, and, on 6th April, he took the life of eighty-year-old Dorthea Hoagland.

Charles was equally active in May. On the 5th, he fatally injected 66-year-old Melvin Simcoe with an anti-coagulant and, a few days later, gave 22-year-old Michael Strenko a lethal dose of norepinephrine. The young man, who had an autoimmune problem, had come to the hospital to have his spleen removed. He had been doing well but suddenly deteriorated. Charles went to speak to his parents, who were anxiously waiting for news in a side ward, and told them that their son would probably die. He was right.

Meanwhile, the police had failed to prove that Charles was a serial killer, their task made difficult by the fact that he often worked on critical care wards where sudden death was to be expected, and there had been no suspicions about foul play when his patients were autopsied. They reluctantly closed the investigation and Charles was free to kill again.

Love my way

Charles Cullen had literally got away with murder and was equally fortunate when his latest girlfriend agreed to move in with – and became pregnant by – him. It was the lonely nurse's opportunity for a new start, but killing was in his blood and he refused to stop.

On 16th June 2003, he injected forty-year-old cancer patient Jin Kyung Han with digoxin. Charles's colleagues managed to resuscitate the mother of two but were baffled when tests showed that she had the drug in her system. They were equally perturbed to find that two bottles of the heart medication were missing from the medical supplies cupboard. Meanwhile, the patient recovered and was sent home, though, three months later, she died of her original illness. (He would later be found guilty of her attempted murder.)

The Very Reverend Florian Gall died the following month, also due to a digoxin overdose. Charles injected the medication into the Catholic priest's IV tube as his relatives sat by his bedside. The 68-year-old went into cardiac arrest and could not be resuscitated. A concerned doctor informed the New Jersey Department of Health and Senior Services that six patients had abnormal drug levels in their systems.

Meanwhile, the emotionally damaged nurse

continued to kill with impunity. Later that summer, he gave eighty-year-old Pasquale Napolitano an overdose of dobutamine, which fatally accelerated his heart rate. Charles's next patient, carpenter Christopher Hardgrove, was only thirty-eight and recovering from a heart attack. On 11th August, he gave the father of two teenage daughters an injection of norepinephrine; he died within hours. The following month, Charles was working the graveyard shift when he murdered seventy-year-old Krishnakant Upadhyay. Three days later, he made a second attempt to kill 83-year-old James Strickland, who had survived a digoxin overdose in August. This time, the accomplished musician died. Alarmed, the hospital hired their own private investigator and subsequently took their findings to the prosecutor.

Unaware that he was now a person of interest, the male nurse killed again, injecting digoxin into the drip bag of 73-year-old hospital volunteer Edward Zizik. He had been married for forty-eight years.

By now, detectives had fully investigated Charles Cullen's psychiatric history – the suicide attempts, the mental cruelty that he'd inflicted on his wife and children, the physical abuse of animals. They also found that he had ordered and taken receipt of drugs at the hospital, then cancelled the orders in the hope of putting investigators off the scent.

At the end of October, Somerset Medical Center fired him, though they said it was because he had lied on his CV.

Charles immediately applied to another hospital for a job but, fortunately, details of the investigation appeared in a local newspaper. Relatives began to phone the police, citing how their own loved ones had died shortly after the nurse injected them...

Arrested

On 12th December 2003, detectives arrested the medic whilst he was out on a date with his girlfriend. The 43-year-old showed no emotion. He refused a polygraph test but soon agreed to talk to detectives about his unhappy childhood and equally miserable adult life.

He told them of his early and later suicide attempts, about being bullied in the navy, about his alcoholism and failed marriage and affairs. To their surprise, he talked with equal candour about his murder spree, saying that he wanted to die but feared death, and found it easier to have a sort of 'death wish by proxy', in which he killed patient after patient. He said that they had been elderly and suffering, that he had put them out of their misery, but this wasn't entirely true.

Some of Charles's patients had been recovering well and were looking forward to resuming their lives in the outside world. His youngest victim, who admittedly had numerous serious health problems, was only twenty-two. Some of them hadn't died when the nurse first poisoned them, so he had watched them suffer, be revived, feel ill and finally recover, only for him to administer another overdose and put them through the same hell again.

Charles was also very good at blaming other people for his problems, which was something he'd done all of his life. He said that security at many hospitals was lax, that no one cared enough to stop him. He'd have given up nursing but he needed the salary so that he could pay child maintenance. He also told detectives that he thought he'd stop killing when he had someone special in his life – but the reality was that he'd continued his murder spree after his girlfriend moved in with him and after she was expecting his child.

The nurse professed to be worried about the impending baby, afraid that people would shun the child because he, Charles, had murdered repeatedly. He confirmed that neither his girlfriend nor his colleagues had been aware that he was a serial killer.

As he had spent so much of his life in therapy,

Charles confided his emotions and personal highs and lows to the detectives. When they steered him back to the murders, he admitted to committing thirty to forty – he'd lost count. He couldn't remember most of the patients' names but, given access to their files, was able to recall which fatal drugs he'd given them, how they'd responded, how their relatives had reacted and so forth. The act of killing and the aftermath were etched in his mind, yet the actual victims were unimportant and he had killed them as emotionlessly as most people kill a fly.

Charles told the police that he wanted to die, so he was put in a padded cell and kept on suicide watch. Meanwhile, investigators ordered that the body of one of his patients, Helen Dean, be exhumed. Although it had been ten years since the nurse allegedly murdered her, they knew that digoxin remains in the tissues for a very long time. Mrs Dean's remains were autopsied and traces of digoxin were indeed present, indicating that Charles Cullen had told the truth.

On 22nd February 2004, the nurse celebrated his forty-fourth birthday in jail. No one visited him. The following month he was moved out of isolation and into the general prison population, where he shared a cell with another prisoner.

Content to keep a low profile, he spent most of his time reading both novels and non-fiction books.

Court hearings

At his first court hearing, Charles admitted to killing thirteen patients at Somerset Medical Center. He said that he had injected them with various drugs with the intention of causing their deaths. Sixty relatives of the murder victims had come to see the murderous medic and many wept but the nurse remained emotionless.

Later, at a hearing in Warren County, he pleaded guilty to three murders at Warren Hospital. He also pleaded guilty to five murders at Hunterdon Medical Center. In total, he pleaded guilty to twenty-nine murders, namely John Yengo, Lucy Mugavero, Mary Natoli, Helen Dean, Leroy Sinn, Earl Young, Catherine Dext, Frank Mazzacco, Jesse Eichlin, Ottomar Schramm, Matthew Mattern, Irene Krapf, William Park, Samuel Spangler, Daniel George, Edward O'Toole, Eleanor Stoecker, Joyce Mangini, Giacomino Toto, John Shanagher, Dorthea Hoagland, Melvin Simcoe, Michael Strenko, Florian Gall, Pasquale Napolitano, Christopher Hardgrove, Krishnakant Upadhyay,

James Strickland and Edward Zizik. He also pleaded guilty to six attempted murders, those of Stella Danielczyk, John Gallagher, Paul Galgon, Jin Kyung Han, Frances Agoada and Philip Gregor, and was cumulatively sentenced to 127 years in prison before becoming eligible for parole. In other words, he was now destined to die in jail.

18   Orville Lynn Majors

A smooth-talker, this nurse initially convinced many people of his innocence. With his hatred of the elderly, he is similar to Britain's Colin Norris.

Early arrogance

Born in 1960, Orville grew into a young man who didn't suffer fools gladly. He referred to those less fortunate than himself as 'wasters' and 'trailer trash' and hated anyone who claimed state benefits. He was bisexual and seemed very comfortable with this.

Death toll

In 1993, the somewhat overweight nurse began working in the intensive care unit at Vermillion

County Hospital in Indiana. Over the next 22 months, 147 patients died, mostly in his care. He made it clear to his peer group that he hated elderly people and told a friend that they should all be gassed. A supervisor noted that the death rate increased whenever Orville was on duty but that it declined when he was away from the unit. As a result, an inquiry was launched and Orville was suspended on full pay. Seven bodies were exhumed but there were no traces of foul play and the nurse was not charged with anything, though he received negative press coverage.

A television star

By 1997, there were sixty lawsuits against Orville Lynn Majors as grieving relatives sought justice. The well-dressed medic appeared on an episode of *The Montel Williams Show,* which was highlighting false criminal accusations, and Orville was so plausible that he won over the host, audience and even a top criminologist. The relatives of several patients said that they'd seen him give medication to their elderly parents and that, moments later, that patient had unexpectedly died, but a plausible-sounding Majors pointed out that people died in hospital all the time.

Nevertheless, detectives were convinced that

they had a case, and, in December of that same year, Orville was arrested and charged with the murder of seven patients. Shortly afterwards, the authorities exhumed another 15 bodies and found that 6 of these deaths were attributable to epinephrine and potassium chloride, which often leave no trace in the body. (Kristen Gilbert also used these drugs to murder patients in her care.) Vials of both drugs were found in Orville's former home and in his van, alongside syringes and other medical paraphernalia that should not have been taken from the hospital.

Trial

Though the licensed practical nurse was suspected in the murder of 130 patients of both sexes, he was only charged with six, the oldest victim being 89 and the youngest 56.

The defence said that the nurse was being scapegoated because the authorities had spent a fortune on the investigation and had to blame someone. Orville himself said that he was taking the brunt of poor practice in his former workplace, that he had always given his patients good care. Several doctors testified for the defence team, stating that these could have been natural deaths.

However, the prosecution produced witnesses who testified that almost twice as many patients had died on Orville's shift as on any other nurse's shift. The other nurses admitted that they even took bets on which of his patients would die next. When the other medics fought to save someone, Orville would often plead, 'Let them die.' On one occasion, he'd been found sitting next to an alert female and another nurse had asked him why he was keeping watch, to which he'd replied that he was waiting for the patient to expire. His nursing colleague was baffled as the woman seemed to have made a good recovery – but, moments later, she died.

Bizarrely, Orville seems to have murdered some patients in front of their sons or daughters. He'd kiss the patient on the head, murmur that there was nothing more to worry about and then inject them. Most died within a moment, much to their relatives' shock.

On 17th October 1999, Orville Lynn Majors was found guilty of murdering six patients and was sentenced to serve 360 years. He showed no emotion, though his sister said that he was being scapegoated and his mother wept, insisting that he hadn't killed anyone. Like most Angels of Death, he has continued to protest his innocence.

PART FOUR

DEADLY DENTISTS

The crimes committed by these dentists were largely up-close and personal. One man was believed to have killed his adoptive daughter after allegedly sexually abusing her, whilst another apparently killed his wife after a furious row. Clara Harris was convicted of deliberately aiming her car at her adulterous husband, moments after finding him at a hotel with another woman. Only the late Glennon Engleman had a financial motive for his murder spree, often persuading his friends to take part in his heinous insurance schemes.

19   Dr Samuel Perera

This dentist was sufficiently arrogant that he convinced himself that he would never be charged with murdering his adopted daughter, despite the fact that he hid some of her body parts in the house.

Early success

Samuel Perera was born in 1943 in Ceylon. A bright child, he went on to study Medicine at Colombo University, specialising in oral biology. Samuel then moved to England and studied at a dental school attached to Newcastle University, enjoying a three-year scholarship.

During his scholarship he met a Hindu woman called Dammika and married her, though he insisted that she convert to his religion, Catholicism. Samuel became a lecturer in dentistry at the Leeds School of Medicine and he and Dammika set up home in Wakefield, where they had two children – both daughters – in the late 1970s.

Samuel's students looked up to him and he expected the same level of hero-worship from his wife and children. He saw himself as superior to all females and expected to be waited on hand and foot.

A slave

In 1981, Samuel decided to adopt a little girl from his native Sri Lanka. He and his wife went out there and bought a ten-year-old girl from an impoverished family who lived in a modest, straw-roofed dwelling. Her name was Nilanthe but he decided to call her Philomena. He referred to her as 'a jungle girl' and police were later convinced that he wanted to raise her as a household slave.

For the next two years, neighbours sometimes saw Philomena with the rest of the family and felt sorry for her as she looked downcast and spoke little English. But, from November 1983 onwards, she was never seen outside. When they enquired about the child's health, Mrs Perera said that Samuel was very strict and that he'd locked the twelve-year-old in a room for making eyes at men.

The months passed and the neighbours grew

even more concerned at the little girl's non-appearance. In April 1984, Mrs Perera said that her husband had sent her back to Sri Lanka to live. Unconvinced, the neighbours contacted police.

Detectives arrived at the Perera household and immediately became aware of the dentist's poor attitude towards women as he angrily ordered his wife and daughters upstairs. He then described taking Philomena to Sicily to visit his brother, after which she'd been put on a plane back to her native land. However, inquiries showed that Perera *hadn't* travelled to visit his brother and Philomena's family hadn't seen her since the informal adoption took place. Police became convinced that the man had murdered the little girl and speculated that he may have sexually assaulted her and feared that she would tell.

Body parts

On 4th February 1985, one of Perera's colleagues was looking in a drawer when he found a human jawbone and pieces of a human skull in a large envelope. A further search revealed three containers of decalcifying fluid with bone fragments inside. Given time, these bones would have disintegrated, leaving no trace.

The shocked man called the police and they

took Samuel Perera into custody. They also began to dig up the garden of his home and soon found a bone, tooth and human hair.

Entering the house, they found three large plant pots containing small, withered geraniums. Examining them more closely, they smelt the sweet stench of decay. One of the officers took the central plant pot outside and gingerly turned it upside down. Entwined in the roots, they found an entire human spine. The other two pots contained lumps of rotting human flesh.

Despite the evidence against him, Samuel Perera was convinced that he could talk his way out of a murder charge. He said that the flesh was pork and that he'd been trying it out as a fertiliser. He tried to explain away the bones in his laboratory by claiming that they were legitimate samples used in his experiments, but forensic tests showed that these were the remains of a girl aged between twelve and fifteen, the former being his adopted daughter's age. The dentist then declared that he'd purchased a body in Sri Lanka and brought it back in his hand luggage for the purposes of dissection. The detectives then travelled to Sri Lanka and interviewed the medical university's authorities, ascertaining that the dentist had never purchased a body there.

At Leeds Crown Court, a jury found him guilty of unlawful killing and on 11th March 1986 he was jailed for life.

20 Dr Clara Harris

Hell hath no fury like a woman scorned, as Clara's husband found to his cost when he cheated on her.

Early bereavement

Clara Suarez was born in 1957 to a Roman Catholic couple in Colombia. Unfortunately, her father died when she was six. This may have left her with a fear of abandonment and goes some way towards explaining her desperate later attempts to save her marriage.

Fortunately Clara's mother ran a successful seamstress business and Clara thrived at school and university. She graduated from dental school and set up her own dental surgery in Colombia, later moving to the United States. She practised dentistry in Houston and even entered a beauty competition in 1991, taking first prize.

Marriage

Happily settled in the United States, Clara fell in love with a fellow dentist, David Harris, and married him on St Valentine's Day, 1992. He had been previously married but had divorced his wife when their daughter, Lindsay, was four.

For many years, Clara and David had a loving relationship. They built up a thriving dental practice that employed fifteen people and were well liked by both patients and staff. Devout Baptists, they often hosted church socials at their palatial home and David played in a Christian band.

They wanted children, but Clara had to endure repeated bouts of fertility treatment before she finally got pregnant. In 1998, to the couple's delight, she gave birth to twin sons. She put on a little weight and obviously had less time to devote to her appearance or to David, especially as one of the boys was asthmatic. She also had a strong temper and liked to get her own way. Over time, her husband began to feel neglected and found himself increasingly attracted to Gail Bridges, their dental receptionist.

David began to work out at the gym, lost twenty pounds, and had a hair transplant. He was more short-tempered with Clara and with the twins but she put it down to the fact that they were having a new clinic constructed, so it was a particularly expensive and anxious time.

But, in the spring of 2002, a friend told her that David was having an affair with Gail, a mother of three who shared his passion for religion. Clara confronted him and he readily admitted it. Clara immediately fired Gail and had a long talk with her husband. Afterwards, the Harrises made love and vowed to make a new start.

Clara decided to rejuvenate herself for David so immediately went on a diet, joined a gym, coloured her hair and planned to have a breast enhancement. It was a lot for a 45-year-old mother of two to go through, but she was determined to keep her man. She also gave up work so that she would have more energy for her marriage and she began to read self-help books.

Desperate to find out something bad about Gail, she hired a private detective agency to carry out surveillance on her. Meanwhile, she bombarded Gail with hate calls and threatened to kill her until Gail was in fear for her life.

On 24th July, the detective agency phoned Clara to say that her husband had booked into one of the bedrooms at a local hotel. Enraged, she drove to the hotel with David's sixteen-year-old daughter Lindsay. Spotting Gail's car in the car park, Clara bent the wipers, scratched the paintwork with her keys and finally etched the word *adulterer*.

She called her husband from her mobile phone, telling him that one of the children was sick and that he had to return home. When he came out of the elevator, holding hands with Gail, Clara attacked her rival, pulling her hair, wrestling her to the ground and even biting her on the leg. Meanwhile, Lindsay hit her father with her bag and told him that she hated him. Hotel staff helped break up the fight and Clara left the building in tears.

She got into the driver's seat of her Mercedes and Lindsay got into the passenger seat – but, instead of leaving the car park, Clara circled around it before driving at David and Gail at top speed. Gail managed to get inside her car but David was hit hard and thrown 25 feet. As he lay there, Clara aimed the car and ran over him three times, reversed, then drove forward over his body again, with Lindsay screaming for her to stop.

When the Mercedes halted, Clara got out and said to her dying husband, 'David, look what you made me do.' She was escorted back into the hotel by horrified staff.

A passerby tried to help David but his ears had been torn off, his ribs were caved in, his pelvis was broken and it was obvious from his breathing that one of his lungs had collapsed. He died shortly afterwards at the local hospital.

Arrest and trial

Clara Harris was swiftly arrested for her husband's murder. By now she'd gone into shock and was semi-conscious. She was bailed and returned to live at the mansion with her twin sons, but David's daughter was devastated by the bereavement and twice tried to commit suicide.

At the trial, Lindsay alleged that Clara had told her, 'I could kill him and get away with it for all he's put me through.' She also claimed that Clara had said, 'I'm going to hit him,' as she aimed the Mercedes at the startled-looking man.

A witness testified that Clara had not been crying or emotional when she got in the car and drove it towards David. Rather, she'd looked angry. Everyone agreed that she'd driven over her husband several times before parking and running over to him as he lay, bleeding and struggling for breath, on the ground. A woman trained in first aid who had approached David in the hope of helping him had heard Clara say, 'David, look what you made me do.'

Clara Harris wept as she heard details of her husband's injuries and became so emotional that the judge, determined not to have histrionics in her courtroom, briefly had Harris removed from the court.

Later, Clara took the stand and described how David had talked in glowing terms about his lover, praising her good communication skills, soft voice, slender body and big breasts. In contrast, he found his wife acerbic and difficult to talk to. She had felt humiliated and hurt.

However the scorned wife was less believable when it came to describing the events in the car park. She said that she'd closed her eyes as she drove, that she didn't mean to hit David and that, afterwards, she couldn't understand why he was lying on the ground.

Questioned by the prosecution, Clara had to admit that she and David had discussed divorce and had talked about a property settlement. He had told her that he wanted her to be happy, that she could have the house and car.

The prosecutor described how Clara had felt towards her husband in the car park and suggested, 'You were angry.'

'No, I was hurt,' Clara replied. But later she

agreed with the lawyer that she had been furious.

The defence concluded that Clara hadn't meant to drive into her husband, and that she deserved to be freed to return to her twins. She had told friends that she would probably commit suicide if she went to prison, but her defence team said that they were sure that the jury would find her innocent.

In summary, the prosecution said, 'If a man is cheating on you, you take him to the cleaners. You take his house, you take his car. But you don't kill him.' Harris had robbed three children of their father and a couple of their son, yet Clara believed she would be found not guilty as her church, community and friends were all praying for her. She said that her deity would not let her go to jail.

The jury returned the following day with a guilty verdict. Clara Harris closed her eyes and was visibly shocked. Later, as her stepdaughter and David's father made their heart-wrenching impact statements, she wept. Five hours later, the jury came back with a sentence of twenty years, whereupon the dentist collapsed and had to be escorted from the court.

Clara Harris is serving out her sentence in Mountain View Prison in Gatesville, Texas, where she sometimes works in the prison's computer laboratory. Her sons are being raised by her former neighbours, though David's parents have visitation rights.

In September 2005, the Texas Court of Criminal Appeals turned down her request for a new trial. She will be eligible for parole after serving ten years.

21   Dr Glennon Engleman

The Engleman case is unusual because Glennon was a dental surgeon who could have made more money from his dental practice than he did from his deadly insurance scams. It's also a bizarre case as he killed in partnership with someone else, although his partners changed from time to time. Finally, the case is extraordinary due to Glennon's belief in astrology, which eventually led him to admit to several of the murders.

Astral projection

Glennon was born on the 6th February 1927 to Frank and Annora Engleman. The family – which included another son and a daughter – lived in St Louis, Missouri. Frank worked long hours as a railroad clerk then came home and drank beer and chewed tobacco. He was a quiet, law-abiding man. Annora, a housewife, had a more critical outlook on life and mocked Frank for paying his utility bills quickly. She believed in astral projection and astrology and told Glennon that she could astrally follow him around. He was her favourite child and she encouraged him to read as voraciously as she herself did, and told him that he could become a professional man.

Unfortunately Glennon's teachers had little faith in him, assuming that he'd become an unskilled worker like his father. He railed against this and got into various clashes at school, so was expelled several times. Despite raising hell as a teenager, he went on to become a qualified dentist and set himself up in practice in an indigent St Louis neighbourhood.

Contradictions

From the start of his professional life, Glennon Engleman was a mass of contradictions. He sometimes treated his hard-working but impoverished patients for free, though he refused to treat anyone that was on welfare. He was proud of his profession yet wasn't very good at it, and as a result his wealthier new patients often got their teeth refilled elsewhere.

Glennon clearly saw himself as a rising star but spent so little on clothes that even his poorest patients noticed, yet he insisted on picking up the tab whenever he took friends or relatives to lunch and was equally generous with his lovers, often giving them cash. He adored his sister so much that he allegedly contributed to the upkeep of her mansion, yet he often failed to pay his taxes and would spend hours doing DIY tasks badly rather than call in a professional.

The dentist was rabidly homophobic, anti-Semitic and racist, yet his mother, whom he adored, was from parents who were half-Cherokee. He boasted that he'd fathered several illegitimate children and often had two or more lovers in his thrall at a time, yet he found pornography offensive and tried to have a local porn store closed down.

Multiple marriages

Despite his aversion to porn, Glennon Engleman was apparently brilliant in bed. He would perform cunnilingus endlessly on his lovers and was equally keen to be fellated. He also had immense staying power and would orgasm twice in a sex session, even when he was in his fifties. Yet he wasn't able to maintain a happy marriage and divorced several times.

His first wife, Ruth, was a student teacher. It was an unusual marriage in that Glennon remained at home with his mother (his father having died) whilst Ruth lived in a flat with several other students. Ruth had enjoyed a party-girl lifestyle yet now she and her young husband were reduced to having sex in his car. Unsurprisingly the relationship broke down, and within three years they were divorced.

Glennon's second wife, Eda, was a librarian. This time he took his bride to live with himself and his mother, who insisted on doing most of the cooking. That relationship also began to break down and Eda told her parents that he'd tried to kill her with barbiturates.

Whilst he was still married to Eda, Glennon started to have an affair with a 21-year-old patient, Ruth Jolley. She remained his girlfriend for several years until he physically threw his wife Eda out of the house.

Ruth now became his third wife (and the second of his wives to be called Ruth) and bore him a son, David, on whom Glennon doted. Glennon's mother died during this marriage so, for the first time, he lived alone with his wife and child. Unfortunately, the relationship soon became rocky with the dentist staying away most weekends. Ruth knew that Glennon kept a special bed in his dental surgery on which to have sex with female patients who were attracted to him.

After this divorce, Glennon went to live with his sister, Melody, and her husband. The siblings were so close that outsiders sometimes thought they were dating. Melody shared their mother's love of the occult and would later declare herself to be a psychic white witch.

A criminal mindset

Glennon Engleman had grown up believing that you had to commit crime to get ahead. As such, he claimed that his boat had been stolen and got the insurance money. In truth, he sank the boat himself, but first reclaimed the expensive motor. He would continue to pursue such 'victimless' frauds – including money laundering – for many years. His mother had encouraged him in this, saying that banks and insurance companies were fair game, that it wasn't stealing. Friends noticed that Glennon became more and more amoral after such mother-son talks.

He would eventually receive lengthy jail sentences for mail fraud and for conspiracy to commit mail fraud, and his third wife, Ruth, would admit to helping him by money laundering.

The first alleged murder

By 1958, Glennon's first wife, Ruth, had married again. Six months after the marriage, her new husband, James Bullock – who was studying accountancy – drove off in the direction of his evening class but his body was later found lying in the road beside his car, which was parked outside a known homosexual haunt. He had been shot in the vehicle and sustained four bullet wounds that had caused profuse bleeding. A man was seen running away from the bloody scene. The witness, a passing driver, called the emergency services, but, moments after James Bullock was stretchered into the ambulance, he died.

When the police found that Ruth was still seeing her first husband, Glennon Engleman, they asked for his alibi. At first he said that he'd been buying his current wife a Christmas present but when this story didn't check out he admitted that he'd been performing an abortion and hadn't mentioned it because it was illegal. The police tried to arrest him for this but he punched the arresting officer, earning a $100 fine. None of his patients would admit that he'd performed abortions on them so the case was closed.

Ruth's insurance claim was contested and it was two years before she received $64,000 from the insurance company. She promptly handed $20,000 of it over to Glennon Engleman to invest. Meanwhile, Glennon told his friends that the attractive Ruth was much better off without her 'faggot' husband. Though heavily suspected of this murder – and linked with it publicly after reports in the local paper – he was never charged. His third wife, also called Ruth, would allege that he told her he'd committed the killing and that he was proud of it.

The second murder

Five years later, in 1963, Glennon Engleman was working on a drag-racing investment. He'd had an affair with a beautiful eighteen-year-old, Sandy, and now persuaded her to marry a young man called Eric Frey. Eric was interested in drag racing and soon got involved with Glennon's drag-racing strip. Meanwhile, the newly-weds took out life assurance schemes.

The marriage wasn't a happy one and the dentist was soon telling his friends that Sandy would be better off without Eric. He told Sandy the exact same thing. Various friends of the dentist also admitted to knowing that Eric Frey was about to die at Glennon Engleman's hands.

On 26th September 1963, Eric, Sandy and several of Glennon's other friends made their way to the drag strip to work there for the evening. Glennon asked Eric to help him blow up a well with dynamite as he was afraid that some of the children who played on the strip would fall in. Eric obligingly approached the well, whereupon Glennon hit him over the head with a rock and threw him down it. Some of the others heard the young man cry out, 'Why do you want to kill me?' but Sandy didn't hear her husband's cries, as she'd walked some distance away. In response, Glennon climbed into the well and held the semi-conscious man's head under the water. Everyone listened to Eric splash and gurgle – then the eventual silence told them that he'd drowned.

Glennon left the well, one of his friends ignited the dynamite and everyone told the police that Eric had accidentally blown himself up. His wife of one year received $25,000 insurance money for this supposedly accidental death and duly handed $16,000 of it over to Glennon for his drag strip. The strip went bankrupt the following year.

The early Sixties was also the time that the dentist acquired a new best friend, Robert Handy. His new friend would assist in some of his murderous crimes...

Robert Handy

Robert Handy was an attractive man who had once been married to a St Louis Playboy Club bunny girl. (When he was finally arrested, he was dating a stripper.) He worked as a carpenter but his main love was nature and animals. He met Glennon when he was working on Glennon's brother Vernon's house.

Robert genuinely seemed to care for Glennon Engleman. The admiration was mutual, with Glennon telling other friends that Robert was as courageous as a lion. The men often drove for long distances together to enjoy the countryside, sometimes taking David, Glennon's son, with them. Robert also had children who'd been left with him after his divorce.

In the early Sixties, the two men were involved in a counterfeiting scheme, and, when the police caught up with Robert, he alone took the rap for it. He was released in September 1968.

The third murder

By the mid-Seventies, Glennon Engleman was again looking for additional funds. This time he turned his attention to Carmen Miranda, his 24-year-old dental nurse. She had known him since she was a little girl, as her impoverished Mexican family helped to clean his house. When she'd become pregnant at seventeen, Glennon had performed an illegal abortion on her, after which she'd almost bled to death, but Carmen remained loyal to Glennon as he was the most intelligent, educated and powerful person that she and her seven siblings had ever known.

Glennon told her that she'd have to pull off some kind of scam if she ever wanted to better herself. He had persuaded her to marry a man called Peter Halm and told her that, if Peter was to die, she'd get the insurance money and could give some of it to him...

In September 1976, Carmen agreed to lure her unsuspecting spouse to a remote picnic area frequented by hunters, knowing that Glennon Engleman and Robert Handy would be waiting for him there. When Peter got close enough, Glennon Engleman raised his rifle, took aim and blasted him in the head. The unfortunate young man collapsed, bleeding profusely, and begged his wife to get help. Seconds later, he died.

As Glennon had predicted, the police weren't too interested in the death of an ordinary working man and the case was put down as an accidental shooting. Carmen received $37,500 from the death but was allegedly so upset that she gave most of it to her brother. Glennon, however, took $10,000, most of which he used to pay his overdue tax bill, but his debts soon mounted up again.

The fourth and fifth murders

The following year, Glennon was once again prepared to kill for profit. By now, he had a lover called Barbara who was divorced. Glennon soon persuaded her to remarry and to insure her new husband. He told her to choose an ordinary man (not a professional man or anyone involved in law enforcement) so that the authorities wouldn't investigate closely when he died.

Shortly after the marriage, Barbara told Glennon that her new in-laws – Arthur and Vernita Gusewelle – were wealthy farmers. Their estate was valued at over half a million dollars, and if they died the money would be divided equally between her new husband, Ronald, and his brother.

Robert Handy and Glennon Engleman drove to the estate on the evening of 3rd November 1977. Glennon knocked at the door and said that he was from the Farm Bureau: as usual, the dentist sounded entirely plausible. It seems that, initially, Robert waited outside in the car.

Once inside the house, Glennon produced his

gun and ordered the couple to lie on the floor. They followed his orders, doubtless hoping that he would spare them, but he shot them both through the head. Vernita, 55, died quickly but her 71-year-old husband, though mortally wounded and blinded, briefly regained consciousness.

Robert Handy now allegedly entered the farmhouse (according to Glennon's testimony and the fact that Arthur Gusewelle said the word 'two' as he was dying) and ransacked it to make it look like a profit-based double murder. They left the scene believing that they were leaving behind two corpses, but Arthur Gusewelle managed to drag himself to the phone after the killers left. He was able to tell the ambulance crew that there were 'two', and they believed that he meant two men. He said 'two' again at the hospital before he died.

However, Glennon Engleman and Robert Handy weren't finished with what Glennon would later describe as 'his biggest project'. They planned to wait for a few months and then kill Barbara's husband, Ronald Gusewelle, so that all of the money went to Barbara, after which Glennon could directly benefit. Eager to make as much from her husband's forthcoming death as possible, Barbara forged his signature on an insurance application form to the tune of $193,000. The pretty woman had become a Black Widow who thought she'd be set up for life.

The sixth murder

By March 1979 the Gusewelles' estate had been divided up and Glennon and Robert decided that it was time that 33-year-old Ronald Gusewelle died. Barbara ushered them into Ronald's garage shortly before he was due home. She also got towels ready to mop up any telltale blood.

Glennon shot the luckless man in the chest as he entered the garage. Uncomprehending for a second, Ronald stood swaying and was promptly bludgeoned with a hammer – Glennon would later say that Robert did the bludgeoning. Robert helped squash Ronald's corpse into his car, breaking one of his legs in the process, then the men drove the car to an area frequented by prostitutes, put condoms in Ronald's pocket and hoped that the death would look like a sexual homicide.

The seventh murder

That same month, a dental laboratory owner called Sophie Marie Berrera found that someone had planted a bomb in her garage. Fortunately the building leaked and the bomb became rain-soaked and didn't detonate.

Sophie had previously filed a law suit against

Glennon Engleman as he owed her $14,500. This was for dental impression work she'd done for him over an extended period. The dental impressions he had handed in were so poorly taken that Sophie had to spend longer on them than on other impressions, and as a result, she tried to charge him more.

Sensing that Glennon was behind the bombing, Sophie dropped her lawsuit but towards the end of the year she filed again. On 14th January 1980 she got into her car and turned the ignition key. The resultant explosion could be heard for miles around. Both of her feet were blown off and there was massive damage to her torso. One of her ears was found a hundred yards away.

Immediately after her death, Sophie's family told the police that Glennon Engleman had hated her and that she'd feared he would kill her. The dentist denied everything so the police went to speak to his third wife, Ruth, with whom he was still having sex. Ruth had already admitted to money laundering for Glennon but now – fearing for her own life – she wanted no more to do with his illegal schemes. She told the authorities about the various murders that the dentist claimed to have been responsible for and she agreed to wear a wire so that they could hear him for themselves. Unlike most murderers, Glennon liked to talk about his killings, albeit in a coded way. He called this 'homicidal intimacy'.

Have you read the news today?

By January 1980, the St Louis *Globe* newspaper was noting that Glennon had benefited from two unsolved murders and a supposedly accidental death: the lawsuit against him had been dropped after Sophie Berrera's murder, and he had benefitted from James Bullock's shooting and from Eric Frey's death in the well because both of their widows had invested money in his drag strip. The dentist was livid when he read the reports but he believed that none of his co-conspirators would betray him. Meanwhile, he had been betrayed by his own body; he had developed diabetes and required frequent medicine.

Trapped by a tape

Eager to make an arrest before the dentist could strike again, the police had been listening avidly to Glennon's many post-coital conversations with his third ex-wife, Ruth. He hinted at various murders and had admitted taking money from his dental nurse Carmen Miranda after her husband's mysterious shooting – but at one stage he went further, saying, 'I have no desire to keep on killing my fellow man.' This, with the masses of circumstantial evidence and financial motives, was enough for the police to make an arrest. First, they moved Ruth and her son to an unknown locale under the Federal Relocation Program. It was a move that may well have saved her life. Glennon Engleman had already hinted that he would kill her when their son became a teenager, suggesting that a teenage boy no longer needs a protective mother – so she was terrified of what he'd do once he knew that she'd betrayed him for many weeks.

Other arrests

In February 1980, the police arrested Glennon Engleman, Robert Handy, Carmen Miranda and her brother Nick Miranda. (Nick had acted as the go-between, handing Engleman $10,000 of the $75,000 Carmen received from the insurance company.) Robert Handy cried when he heard that Glennon had been arrested and originally refused to say anything incriminating about his friend. So the police offered Carmen and Nick Miranda immunity from prosecution if they would tell what they knew about Peter Halm's murder, Sophie Berrera's murder and any other crimes that Glennon was being investigated for. The Mirandas also had to agree to testify against Glennon Engleman and Robert Handy in court.

The trials

At first Glennon continued to deny everything and refused to see a psychiatrist, which made things difficult for his defence team. He told friends that he could astrally project himself out of prison whenever he wanted to, so he was very popular with other prisoners, most of whom were equally keen to astral-project.

At his first trial, in Minnesota in 1980, he pleaded not guilty to the murder of Peter Halm but Carmen Miranda testified against him, explaining that the dentist had encouraged her to marry Peter and lure him to the caves where Engleman and Handy would be waiting with their guns.

The prosecution said that Carmen was guilty of murder too but that giving her immunity had been necessary to build a strong enough case against Dr Engleman. She'd suffered from such serious depression after the shooting that she'd been hospitalised and she cut a pathetic figure on the stand. Glennon, who'd known her since she was a baby, wept during her testimony.

The tapes of Glennon and Ruth talking about death were introduced but the judge said that the jury couldn't have a transcript of what was said. Glennon cheered up markedly at this as some of the homicidal pillow talk was somewhat indistinct.

He looked affable in his suit and tie when he took the stand but was clearly enraged at being addressed as Mr Engleman. 'It's *Dr* Engleman,' he corrected immediately.

He admitted that he owned many guns and was an expert shot but denied shooting Peter Halm, so the prosecution asked him why he'd talked to Ruth about committing homicide. Glennon replied that he'd been talking about murder in general terms in order to scare her. And why did he want to frighten her? Because she'd allegedly stolen his coin collection and he wanted it back. He said that he also wanted to scare her into letting him see more of David, who he feared was unduly influenced by her overprotective ways. During this diatribe against his ex-wife he became so incensed that his face turned purple and his eyes bulged. 'That bitch has taken him out of my life,' he growled.

With Carmen Miranda explaining how the murder plot had been formed, Glennon Engleman's guilty sentence was a foregone conclusion. He was sentenced to fifty years without the possibility of parole.

The dentist appeared unconcerned at the verdict, stating, 'I'm fifty-three years old. In fifty years there won't be anything but dust. I don't relish this guilty verdict but we will appeal.'

However, his sentencing days weren't over for he was now sentenced to thirty years for a federal mail fraud and another thirty years for federal bombing charges relating to Sophie Berrera's car bomb murder. Dynamite had been used in the car bomb, which meant that the Alcohol, Tobacco and Firearms agency were involved, and they relentlessly pursued the case.

Meanwhile, Robert Handy was found guilty of mail fraud and of conspiring to commit mail fraud, and was sent to jail. He still wasn't being tried for his part in any of the murders as he refused to talk for fear that he would compromise Glennon Engleman, his dearest friend.

The deadly dentist's trials were continuing. He was tried for the murder of Sophie Berrera, but this ended in a mistrial, at which he told the press that his horoscope showed his betrayal at the hands of a woman (presumably Ruth Jolley, though it could also have been Carmen Miranda) had been predestined at his birth. He added that his sister had drawn up his chart and this showed he would spend the last years of his life with the criminal underworld. He seemed to genuinely believe that the stars had preordained his fate, rather than looking at the truth of the matter – that he'd opted to lure various men and one woman to their deaths in order to both enjoy killing them and benefit financially.

His second trial for the Berrera killing ended in a guilty verdict, but he was given a life sentence rather than the death penalty because he hadn't actually planted the bomb himself, hiring an unnamed source to do that.

Robert Handy's convictions

Robert Handy's verdict was overturned on appeal but he was convicted again by another jury in a retrial in 1985 and sentenced to seventeen years. He aged visibly and lost weight over the next few months, then let it be known that he had information on three murders and would share that information in return for the possibility of a reduced sentence. He also smuggled out a letter to Glennon apologising for the negative things he'd have to say about him.

The police visited Handy in jail, where he admitted that he might have had prior awareness of the Peter Halm murder. He said that he'd feared Glennon would kill him too if he tried to talk Carmen out of it. He also said that he'd tried to talk the dentist out of Sophie Berrera's car bombing. Telling Robert that they needed more detailed information (which he wasn't yet ready to provide as he only wanted to talk to the deal-makers), the police left.

The authorities later explained to Robert that they intended to seek two death penalties for the Gusewelle murders. One would be Glennon Engleman – and the other would either be Barbara Gusewelle or Robert Handy himself.

Robert paled – and then he started talking. He talked for two and a half hours, admitting that Barbara had only married Ronald Gusewelle at Glennon's instigation, knowing that Glennon would kill the man and get the insurance policy, but that she had then discovered he was heir to his parents' fortune and Glennon had decided to kill them first. For a year and a half, Robert Handy, Glennon Engleman and Barbara Gusewelle had discussed how and where to kill Ronald's parents and her husband. Eventually they had the details figured out.

After making a dummy run, Glennon went to Robert's house and the two men took Robert's car to the farmhouse. During the journey, Glennon told Robert that Ronald beat Barbara (this appears to have been a falsehood) and that he consequently deserved to die. Apparently he didn't deserve to die, however, until his parents had been murdered and their wealth had passed on to him...

The dentist stopped at a phone booth and called Barbara, who duly sent her children over to the Gusewelles on an errand, checking that they were home. They were, and the dentist shot them and ransacked the house. According to Handy he remained in the car throughout the double murder, but Glennon would later say that Robert had helped to trash the house. (Also, Arthur Gusewelle had said the word 'two' following the assault.) Robert now told the police that Glennon had promised him he'd get money from the Gusewelles estate – but the promised cash never materialised.

After this double murder, according to Robert, the dentist had started to think up various ways of murdering Ronald Gusewelle. At first he thought he might flag the man down on the road, acting as if he had car trouble. (James Bullock may have been killed by such a con trick.) Then he considered tying Barbara up and getting her to say that there had been a robbery during which her husband had been shot dead.

Finally deciding to murder Ronald Gusewelle in his own garage, Robert said that he and Glennon had driven there and waited with Barbara Gusewelle's blessing. Robert said that he had felt nervous but that Glennon was calm. In his version of events the dentist did both the shooting and the bludgeoning, whereas the dentist said that Robert had been the one who used the sledgehammer to make sure that the man was dead.

The two men had then stuffed Ronald's corpse into his own car whilst Barbara staunched the blood from his head wound and cleaned up the blood that had already been spilt.

As he'd cooperated with the police, Robert Handy was allowed to plead guilty to the lesser charges of conspiracy to murder. He received fourteen years for three counts of conspiracy, to be served concurrently. These three sentences were also concurrent with the seventeen-year sentence he was serving for mail fraud and conspiracy charges on the Peter Halm murder.

Barbara Gusewelle is arrested

By August 1984, the authorities were ready to arrest Barbara Gusewelle for her part in her husband's murder. They found her with her boyfriend and grown-up children enjoying a beach holiday at Lauderdale-by-the-Sea. Three days after her arrest she spent her forty-second birthday in a Florida courtroom. She maintained a blank expression throughout her trial, but Robert Handy apologised to the court for his part in the murders and told the jury that Glennon had many good qualities. For the second time he had a letter smuggled out of prison in which he apologised to his friend, saying, 'You've been like a brother to me.'

The jury were out for fourteen hours, then they returned and found Barbara Gusewell not guilty of her in-laws' murders, but guilty of her husband's murder. She wept. Later she was sentenced to fifty years.

Engleman gives it up

Glennon Engleman was now expected to go to trial for the three Gusewelle murders, but he asked Barbara's lawyer what birth sign he was, and when the man replied Scorpio, Glennon said, 'I always have a bad time going against Scorpios.' Later, he told the authorities to forget the trial, that he was willing to plead guilty to all three of the murders. He was given three life sentences without the possibility of parole.

The myths

The most abiding myth that has come out of the Engleman case is that he killed his female patients if they couldn't pay him, but the reverse is true

– he let very poor patients off with their bills or told them to pay him when they could. He didn't victimise his patients. Rather, he was revered by many of them. The fact that he worked in tandem on several of the homicides has also largely been forgotten so that he's simply described on various crime Internet sites as a male serial killer – but he couldn't have killed Peter Halm without Carmen Miranda, who lured the man to his death and collected the insurance money. Robert Handy was also present at the shooting. Similarly, he had Robert Handy with him when he shot Ronald Gusewelle, and Glennon later alleged that Robert had struck the hammer blow as the already-injured Ronald fell to the garage floor. Robert also admitted to driving to the Gusewelles' farmhouse knowing that the couple were about to be shot, and Glennon's testimony plus that of Arthur Gusewelle himself put Robert inside the house.

The rationale

The homicidal dentist's motives have proved difficult for criminologists to unravel. Superficially, these were murders for profit, but he was so vague about the financial side of things that he benefited very little. Glennon had expected to get more than $16,000 from Peter Halm's shooting, but one of the young man's policies was still in his mother's name rather than in his wife's, and Glennon only netted $4,000 from Barbara Gusewelle for murdering all three Gusewelles because of legal complexities.

Glennon refused to see a psychiatrist but a law enforcement officer suggested that he was psychotic. Psychosis, however, implies a serious mental illness where the person withdraws from reality – in contrast, Glennon Engleman functioned in an entirely rational way. Psychotics also tend to have impaired relationships with people, yet Glennon was close to his mother, sister and ex-wives and had several close friends.

Other crime writers have suggested that the main motive was power, and this is the most likely reason for the seven homicides. It was clearly vital for Glennon Engleman – the son of an unskilled man, seriously underestimated at school – to feel important, superior to those around him. As such, he encouraged impoverished patients to rely on him. Some clearly regarded him as godlike and sang his praises to their friends.

Glennon saw his dental nurse, Carmen Miranda, and her siblings, poor Mexicans, as being inferior to himself. He helped them but he also patronised them. Again, this doubtless made him feel significant. His mother also suggested that he tended to 'marry down'.

The dentist was equally keen to make an impression when it came to friendship. He was generous to his friends in social situations and was always trying to involve them in business ventures in which they would benefit.

This amount of power, however, still wasn't enough, so the dentist turned to the occult, deluding himself into believing that he could leave his body and travel around the countryside. Yet, after these supposed out-of-body experiences, he was still a slightly overweight, balding man in a cheap suit.

Planning murder after murder changed all that. Suddenly he had the power to decide if someone lived or died. He chose death for his first victim and enjoyed the experience. Later he'd admit to police that he liked to kill. Indeed, he liked it so much that he would do so again and again.

As he murdered as part of a couple, Glennon was able to feel powerful for months whilst talking about the proposed murders, then enjoy talking about the deed after it was done. He was angry when Carmen Miranda tried to change the subject in the weeks leading up to her husband's death, telling Robert Handy that she'd become moody and was far too delicate. In contrast, he remained enthralled by his lover and co-conspirator Barbara Gusewelle, telling friends that she would never kiss and tell.

Robert Handy would later tell the authorities that Glennon was excited in the hours leading up to a murder. Glennon retained that excitement for many months afterwards by talking about the deaths with his ex-wife Barbara, often after sex.

His mindset was sufficiently skewed that he saw the murder of innocent people as something positive, telling other prisoners that not everyone had the courage to kill. The fact that some of the wives no longer wanted their husbands seems to have been enough of an excuse for him to commit murder – and he conveniently ignored the fact that these men had parents, siblings and friends who would mourn for the rest of their lives.

Death

The Eighties passed and Glennon Engleman gradually faded from the headlines. He continued to believe in astral projection, but his body remained very much in Jefferson City Correctional Center. There he received regular treatment for his diabetes and died of natural causes in the prison infirmary in April 1999. He was seventy-one.

Robert Handy's name also faded from the public memory – and when a documentary was made about the case, he was given a pseudonym.

When Barbara Gusewelle had served twenty

years of her fifty-year sentence for the murder of her husband, Ronald, she asked for clemency. In the interim, she had returned to her previous married name of Barbara Boyle. Ronald's brother, however, (who, of course, had lost his parents as well as his brother thanks to Barbara and Glennon) protested, saying that life should mean life, so she remained incarcerated.

22   Dr Kenneth Taylor

A successful dentist, Taylor had a terrifying propensity for violence, as the women in his life soon found to their cost.

A religious upbringing

Kenneth was born in 1948, the first child of Jean and Zach Taylor. Jean gave up her beautician's job and went on to have two more children whilst her husband worked in a hardware store and attended business college at night. The couple were Baptists though Ken would later say that his mother was the deeply religious one.

When Ken was five, the Taylors moved to a rural part of Cincinnati and he joined the boy scouts, where his parents became scoutmaster and den mother. It sounded claustrophobic but

Ken later described it as ideal and said that he had the perfect childhood, though he became a nail-biter between the ages of eight and nine, when his father seemed more interested in his younger brother than himself. He played baseball and basketball because he believed that excelling at athletics earned him his father's approval and attention. A tall and slim young man, he did well with girls and lost his virginity at sixteen.

At university, he studied Medicine but switched to Dentistry in his second year. Afterwards, some of his acquaintances claimed that his grades hadn't been quite good enough to become a doctor but Ken himself claimed that he'd become emotional when viewing the bodies of two dead children in the mortuary and realised that he couldn't cope with such daily death. He switched to Dental School at Indiana University and easily passed his exams, being sponsored by the Navy throughout his dental course.

First marriage

Ken had a lot of casual sex, and then, on impulse, asked one of his girlfriends, Lynn, to marry him. He was only twenty-one but liked the idea of settling down. Unfortunately, the reality was more mundane and he soon reverted to the lifestyle of a free man. At the time, drugs were readily available in the student subculture and Ken soon succumbed to them. He experimented heavily with acid, marijuana, uppers and downers, and when Lynn got a teaching job in another city, he began to date again as if he were a bachelor.

He was shocked to find, in November 1973, that Lynn was expecting their baby and told her that she'd have to move out. Much to the consternation of his parents, who liked and admired Lynn, Ken later said that the baby wasn't his. When she was in her ninth month of pregnancy he walked out on her and she never saw him again. They quickly divorced.

Second marriage

By now, Ken was dating the woman who would become his second wife, Rosalind, an air stewardess. They married on 14th December 1974, though she disapproved of his drug-taking. Aware of this, he began to cut down, but there was a weakness in him, an inability to face up to life's challenges, so when he crashed their car he abandoned it and reported it stolen. He was arrested for filing a false police report.

In the summer of 1975, he graduated. Immediately afterwards he reported to the submarine base in Groton, Connecticut. By now, he was falling out of love with his second wife so made up a threesome with his new dental nurse and her friend. He began to sleep around, just as he had with his first wife, and also returned to taking drugs, including amphetamines.

In June 1978, he left Rosalind, then reunited with her and initially seemed pleased in December when she announced that she was expecting his baby. However, he continued to take uppers and allegedly stole several hundred dollars she had been saving to buy baby clothes. The couple had an enormous argument in April and Ken punched the fridge so hard that he fractured his hand and had to go to the hospital. A nurse patched him up and he took her out on a date the following night, conveniently forgetting that he was a married man.

Later that same month, Rosalind awoke to find Ken holding a chloroform-soaked pad over her mouth. (Chloroform can be legitimately used to sedate people, but if too much is applied, or the person is particularly susceptible, it can cause unconsciousness or death. It is also used to put animals down.) She twisted about desperately on the bed and the dentist seemed to belatedly come to his senses and apologised. Afterwards the couple prayed together for guidance.

Rosalind also called the Navy chaplain and Ken was counselled by the Navy psychiatrist, who considered him to be a homicidal maniac. He formed the opinion that Ken had never dealt with his problems, that he let everything build up until he snapped. Ken indicated that his father seemed most interested in his athletic abilities and that his mother interfered a great deal in his life. The therapist found that he had a passive-submissive personality and could not handle fear or rage.

Unsure what to do, Rosalind reported the incident to the police, explaining that she didn't want to press charges but did want to make it a matter of record. The police, however, went ahead and arrested Ken on an attempted murder charge.

Meanwhile, a second psychiatrist had decided that Ken's drinking and drug use had caused the violent incident, that he would recover after treatment for his addictions. His wife still didn't want to go to court so the charge against Ken was dropped and the case was sealed.

In summer 1979, she gave birth to the couple's first child, a daughter, but the marriage continued to deteriorate and the dentist had many more affairs.

Third marriage

It was obvious that Ken and Rosalind were not going to live happily ever after so he began looking around for a new love object and found

Teresa Benigno, who applied for a job as his dental hygienist in September 1980. She was only twenty-one, whilst Ken was thirty-two, but insecure men often target younger women. In the same time frame, he slept with other women and even one of his patients – a breach of trust.

Teresa got pregnant and Ken angrily asked if it was his. She slapped his face and he apologised for doubting her, but he wasn't yet divorced so she went ahead and had an abortion. Rosalind also became pregnant by Ken and aborted the foetus.

On 10th July 1983, Ken and Teresa married in Acapulco and honeymooned there, but they did not return on the scheduled flight back to Kennedy Airport. Ken later phoned her parents to say that two men had broken into their hotel room and beaten them, and that the local police had locked him in a holding cell but he had managed to bribe his way out.

Teresa's parents flew to Acapulco and found her in a hospital ward with terrible injuries. Her jugular had been slashed, her front teeth were broken and her eyes badly blackened. Tranquillised by the nursing staff, she claimed that she didn't know what had happened; she appeared to suffer from amnesia. Meanwhile, Ken's business partners in his dental practice alleged that he had stolen thousands of dollars and they angrily dissolved the partnership.

Later, Ken told another woman at the hotel that he and Teresa had had a row, that he had beaten her and she was in the hospital. He also told her that he had spent four days in jail but Teresa had decided not to press charges against him.

Another child

Ken soon found work in a new practice, though he continued to treat patients whilst he was stoned or drunk. He claimed that cocaine helped him to relax and said that the job was unbearably dull if he wasn't taking drugs. He and Teresa moved into a new house – she had remained withdrawn since the shocking incident on their honeymoon – and decided to have a child together. In June 1984 she delivered a healthy baby boy. Ken wrote her a love letter and went overboard on the celebrations but he continued to sleep with Rosalind, his ex-wife. The following month he took out life insurance on Teresa with her blessing: the money would be used to pay for a live-in babysitter if anything happened to her.

On 11th November of that year, Teresa failed to meet a friend. On the 12th, a Monday, Ken phoned her parents and said that she had a bad drug problem, and that she had gone away for a while to get herself sorted out. He had taken her to the airport but she had refused to give him her destination. Bewildered by this story, as Teresa hadn't shown any signs of addiction, her parents insisted that he report her disappearance to the police.

Friends visited the house and found a half-eaten cake, unboxed, on the kitchen counter, left there from several days before. This just wasn't typical behaviour for the house-proud Teresa. Even more bizarrely, her house and car keys were in their usual place. The only unusual thing about the house was the fact that some grey carpet in the spare room had been removed.

Body found

On 15th November, a birdwatcher was walking through a remote sanctuary fifty miles from the New Jersey border, when he found a woman's body wrapped in a piece of grey carpet inside a sleeping bag. She had been badly beaten about the face and head. Police investigated and found that she had been killed elsewhere, as there was little blood at the dump site, and that the cause of death was repeated blows to the head. They were confident that she'd soon be identified as she was wearing several pieces of distinctive jewellery.

Two days later, she was identified as Teresa

Taylor by her father and brother. Ken sounded distraught when he was informed of his wife's death over the phone.

Detectives went to the house and found an earring with dried blood on it in the garage. It matched the other earring on Teresa's corpse. In the interrogation room, a detective said, 'I think that you killed your wife,' and Ken broke down and admitted he had. He said that he'd been provoked, that he'd walked into the nursery to find Teresa fellating Philip, their infant son.

According to the violent dentist, his wife had been touching herself whilst sexually abusing the infant. He'd run downstairs and she'd followed him and leapt on him, striking out with a dumbbell from their home gym. He'd grabbed an unweighted dumbbell and smashed her on the head with it but she'd been so high on cocaine that it hadn't had any discernable effect. He'd struck her again as she went for him with renewed fury, then felt shock when he realised she was dead.

He had put her body in the boot of her car, cleaned up the mess and had driven for many miles, staying overnight with his baby in a motel room. The following day he visited his parents, leaving the body in the boot of the car. He drove on to his ex-wife Rosalind's house and spent the night with her, though she noticed that he looked preoccupied. Finally driving to Pennsylvania, he saw the signs for the bird sanctuary and dumped Teresa's corpse.

The investigation

Detectives applied luminol to the Taylors' house and were able to ascertain that a body had been dragged across the floor from the back room to the garage. The luminol also revealed bloody footsteps and handprints that someone had tried very hard to clean up. They talked to Rosalind and she told them about the chloroform incident.

The Taylors' phone records revealed that someone in their house had phoned several sex lines on the night of the murder and Ken said that Teresa had done so. The police asked him why she'd had Vaseline smeared around her anus and vagina and he said that she'd done that to herself, that she was fondling herself whilst performing a sex act on their five-month-old son.

Later, police looked at the couple's historical phone records and found that someone had called a brothel three times whilst Teresa was in hospital giving birth – and that the same brothel had been phoned three times on the night of her murder. Clearly, Teresa couldn't have made the first set of calls...

Ken agreed to take a lie detector test, during which he was injected with the truth serum, sodium amytal. As the drug took effect, he answered more loquaciously, admitting that he'd planned to rape his second wife Rosalind after chloroforming her. He had never mentioned this as a motive before. Later, he said that he might have psychosexual difficulties and he referred to 'the Acapulco thing,' where Teresa had been brutally beaten up. The doctor administering the test said, 'You said that people had broken in,' and Ken opened his eyes and said, 'That's right.' He continued to assert that Teresa had sexually abused their child, but some people manage to lie whilst under the influence of the drug so any information given isn't admissible in a Jersey court.

Detectives now tracked down Ken's first wife, Lynn, and she described an incident after they'd separated when he'd come to the apartment and thrown a basketball with such force that it broke the back of a wooden chair. They also spoke at length to a witness who had been at the Acapulco hotel and had befriended Teresa and Ken. The latter had said that he and his wife had had an argument and that he'd beaten her. Paramedics called to the scene had found that she'd been brutalised so badly that she had lost control of her bowels. Ken had believed she was dead but the ambulance crew had found a slight heartbeat and rushed her to hospital. They had also examined Ken, who claimed to have been attacked by male intruders, but he only had a few light scratches on his forearms and a tiny red mark on his head.

Trial

The dentist's trial began on 30th May 1985. The prosecution alleged that Ken had killed his wife and dumped her body, then spent time at a topless bar. They dismissed the theory that she had been high on cocaine and had sexually abused their son; only a tiny recreational amount of the drug had been found in her system. The defence, however, noted that the drug wears off quickly. They admitted that the dentist had misled the police in reporting his wife as a missing person and fabricating stories about her disappearance but described her death as 'a family tragedy'. They said that Ken had been defending himself and his baby when he had struck his wife repeatedly over the head.

The defence had an expert take the stand to testify that there was no injury to the victim's genitalia and no sperm in her cavities. Despite the presence of lubricating Vaseline, she had not had sex. The prosecution wondered if Ken had lost his erection and become enraged but it was pure supposition on their part.

The jury was shown a video of the young mother playing with her baby, after which many had tears in their eyes. They also heard from Rosalind about the chloroform attack. Ken took angry, immature notes throughout the trial, writing, 'Maybe I'll come out of this trial with a minimum sentence to serve. Then what? You know that I'll come back to see my girl...' He was referring to his daughter, but ended the note, 'Goddamn you, Rosalind.' It was a chilling insight into a puerile but rage-filled mind.

The testimony about the incident in Acapulco was also damning. Ken alleged that both he and Teresa had been beaten up by intruders, that afterwards he'd crawled over to where his wife lay, covered in blood, on the floor, and had taken her pulse. He'd proceeded to look over the balcony to see if he could locate the culprits and had fainted. When he regained consciousness, he'd washed his legs. Ken wanted to testify but his legal team talked him out of it. The jury were out for two days and returned to find him unanimously guilty of her murder.

In September, he returned to court for sentencing and was given a minimum of thirty years but he was determined not to serve this. The following year, he managed to saw through a window bar, using a smuggled hacksaw, and was close to escaping when the attempt was discovered and shortly afterwards he was moved to a higher security New Jersey jail. A year later, he was suspected of masterminding another escape and was sent to a tougher prison in Virginia. He made further bids for freedom, each resulting in a period of solitary confinement, before settling down. It is likely he will be in his mid-sixties before he is eligible for parole.

PART FIVE

LETHAL PARAMEDICS

These profiles delineate bizarre thinking patterns. Gavin Hall killed the child that he loved in order to wreak revenge on his wife, whilst Kristin Rossum allegedly murdered her husband (whom she could just as easily have divorced) in order to pursue a work-based affair. Bruce Moilanen's motives were ugly but understandable as he benefited financially from his wife's death. Chante Mallard is hard to fathom, for she let a man die rather than spend some time in jail on a drink-driving charge.

Though this paramedic loved his baby daughter, he chose to kill her in order to devastate his estranged wife.

Adultery

Hospital radiographer Gavin Hall met his wife Karen, a cardiac nurse, whilst they were both medical students. They married in 1999 and set up home together in Irchester, Northampton, but the relationship later began to break down.

In September 2005, Karen logged on to an Internet dating site for swingers and was soon exchanging naked photographs with another libertarian, a deputy district judge who was also married. She met him for two sex sessions in a hotel.

In October 2005, Gavin found out about the

affair by reading some of Karen's sexually explicit emails, began to suffer from depression and was given time off work. At some point during this time he decided to hurt her as deeply as possible by murdering their two children, three-year-old Amelia, known as Millie, and baby Lucy. He hadn't originally wanted children but doted on Millie, a daddy's girl, though he had never bonded with her younger sister.

On 26th or 27th November 2005, in what might have been a practice run, he chloroformed two of the three family cats to death – despite the fact that he had previously referred to them as his 'babies' – and hid their bodies in the family shed.

Bizarre behaviour

On 29th November, a mere two days before Millie's fourth birthday, Gavin waited until his wife and Lucy were asleep upstairs in the marital bedroom before bringing the cats' corpses into the lounge and surrounding them with the children's toys. He wanted Karen to come downstairs in the morning to a scene of unimaginable horror.

Gavin gave Millie one of his antidepressants, waited until she was asleep, and then suffocated her with a cloth soaked in chloroform whilst holding her in the crook of his arm. He pressed the cloth hard against her face, leaving scratch marks on her skin. He also strangled her before putting her under a duvet on the lounge floor.

Leaving a previously written suicide note next to the dead child and cats, he sent a text message to his sleeping wife, telling her what he'd done. Finally, he slashed his wrists and chloroformed himself.

Karen came downstairs the following morning to find her oldest daughter and the cats dead, surrounded by teddy bears, and a rambling suicide note filled with quotations from Shakespeare. Her husband was bleeding heavily and unconscious. She called the emergency services and he was revived, arrested and charged.

The radiographer pleaded guilty to manslaughter but denied murder, stating that he was suffering from diminished responsibility. Spectators were angry that Karen's emails were read out in court, noting that her affair in no way justified her husband's homicidal act.

Gavin Hall wept at his trial – held at Northampton Crown Court in November 2006 – when listening to the details of his beloved elder daughter's death. He was jailed for life and told that he must serve a minimum of fifteen years.

Karen later paid tribute to Millie and said that she would plant a cherry tree in their village to honour her memory.

24 Kristin Rossum

As she became increasingly addicted to methamphetamine, this toxicologist resented her husband for standing in her way.

Ruined dreams

Kristin Rossum was born on the 25th October 1976 to Constance and Ralph Rossum, a market researcher and university professor respectively. She was their first child but they went on to have two sons. At the time of Kristin's birth the family lived in Memphis, but they moved around the country to further their careers and by the time Kristin started school, they were living in Maryland.

Kristin studied ballet and wanted to be a dancer, even moving to an Episcopalian boarding school to be near the best dance troupe. (Her parents were devout Episcopalians.) She showed exceptional promise and was allowed to dance with the Boston Ballet during one exciting summer holiday. However, in her mid-teens, Kristin tore several ligaments and had a bad stress fracture, which led to a lot of downtime, during which she gave up on her dream and began to use alcohol. Her self-esteem plummeted and she thought she was overweight and began to take diet pills. By sixteen, she was experimenting with crystal meth. In the short term, it made her feel confident and happy, but, as she continued to use it, she felt ill and tired.

Domestic violence

Kristin's parents went on holiday, leaving Kristin in charge and, when they returned, they found that she had hosted a wild party and that a cheque book and credit cards were missing. They also found a suspicious-looking white powder in their mailbox and her father found a glass pipe and razor blades in her bag.

Kristin told her school counsellor that she wasn't close to her mother and that her dad had grabbed her to prevent her leaving the house. She showed him a bruise on her arm and he duly reported the matter to the police.

The family had a heart-to-heart talk and the seventeen-year-old promised that she wouldn't use drugs again. Returning to 'dutiful daughter' mode, she took up choir singing. But, within weeks, it was obvious that she was once again smoking meths. Her parents called the authorities, who arrested her and put her in a cell for a couple of hours.

She was soon released into her parents' care and they enrolled her at a university thirty miles away. They also went to family therapy in an area where no one knew them. Everything seemed fine until the Rossums arrived to bring Kristin home for the Christmas holiday, only to find that she wasn't there.

Escape

Unable to face the holidays without drugs, Kristin and a group of friends travelled to Tijuana, just over the Mexican border. There, she met Greg de Villers, a college student. They had sex the night they met, after which Kristin moved in with him and his flatmate, though she didn't pay rent. It soon became apparent that she was using drugs but Greg loved her and was convinced that she could turn her life around.

For a while, it seemed that she had. She enrolled

at a different university and studied chemistry, getting good grades, and in June 1997, she took a summer job at the Medical Examiner's Office as an assistant toxicologist and they were very impressed with her. The office stored impounded drugs in evidence envelopes when they were believed to have been connected with a suspicious death, so it was an ideal place for a drug addict. But none of her colleagues or fellow academics were, as yet, aware of Kristin's problem. Nor were her academic tutors, and, the following year, she was voted Most Outstanding Chemistry Student at university.

Marriage

In June 1999, Kristin married Greg, though friends privately thought that she was partially trying to please her parents, who'd virtually adopted him as their third son. By the end of the year, she was complaining that he was clingy, though her spirits revived in January the following year when she found that she'd earned a good degree.

In March, a married toxicologist called Michael Robertson joined Kristin's workplace and there was an immediate spark between them. That same month, Kristin became a full-time employee at the Medical Examiner's Office and the two spent a great deal of time together. By May, they were having an affair.

Later that summer, Greg found one of Michael's many love letters to Kristin. Furious, he phoned the man and warned him to stay away from his wife. That October, Michael's wife left him and the affair escalated. Greg may have confronted Kristin about her drug-taking at this time, telling her that, if she didn't stop, he would inform her workplace. She would lose her job, and her daily access to Michael, unless Greg wasn't around to carry out his threat...

Sudden death

In early November 2000, Greg began to complain of feeling unwell and, on the morning of the 6th, Kristin phoned his workplace and said that he was sick. She went to work looking tired and upset, and left the office several times saying that she was going to check on Greg. On her return, she still looked emotional and withdrawn. She also spent some time with Michael and, after she left his office, her co-workers thought that they saw traces of tears.

At 9.22 p.m., she called the emergency services to say that her husband wasn't breathing. They raced to the scene to find Greg lying on the floor as the emergency operator had told Kristin to put him there in order to do CPR. His torso was sprinkled with red rose petals and others were scattered on the carpet in a scene reminiscent of the film *American Beauty*. Although the paramedics made heroic attempts to revive the 26-year-old, they could not restart his heart.

Questioned by police, Kristin said that she'd told Greg she was leaving him and that he'd later admitted to taking some painkillers and sedatives. She'd come home at teatime and he was warm and breathing, but, at 9.20 p.m., she said that she'd found him dead. She added that he must have sprinkled the rose petals on and around his own body, that they were from a bunch he'd bought her earlier that month. Detectives also found one of the couple's wedding photos under Greg's pillow, and she said that he must have put it there – but these aren't the kind of feminine gestures a no-nonsense young man like Greg would typically make.

Detectives later read Kristin's diary, in which she revealed that she believed she'd married too young and wanted to leave Greg. It was obvious from her writing that *she* was the type to sprinkle rose petals around and she was always demanding that Greg send little notes and similar proofs of his love. They gained the impression that the diary had been written for others to read, that it didn't represent the truth.

Suspicion

As the police investigated further, their suspicions grew. Tests showed that Greg had been dead for some time before Kristin called for medical help, so why hadn't she found him sooner? She said that he'd committed suicide but everyone who knew Greg testified that he wasn't the type to take his own life. He'd also hated prescription drugs of any kind.

They spoke to Michael, who admitted sadly that Kristin was using crystal meth again. Her bosses now moved her into an administrative role as she was no longer a suitable candidate to work with drugs. Shortly afterwards, to no one's surprise, she and Michael were fired.

On 4th January 2001, detectives searched Kristin's house and found meth and drug paraphernalia. She was also under the influence of the drug. To her surprise, she was arrested for using and possession, but was soon bailed.

A murder charge

Shortly afterwards, tests revealed that Greg had died of the drug fentanyl, a controlled substance that Kristin had access to at work and which she was very familiar with. That summer, the police arrested her for his murder and she was jailed until her family posted $1.25 million bail.

Her trial opened in October 2002. By now, investigators had found that she'd bought a rose on the day her husband died, although they couldn't ascertain if it was a red rose or one of a different colour. She'd also spent money on lingerie, doubtless to impress Michael. It was odd behaviour for a young wife whose husband was alone at home feeling so unwell.

Greg's relatives testified that he hadn't been suicidal and that he'd hated prescription medication. He wasn't even much of a drinker, so to have taken an overdose of a controlled drug would have been completely out of character for him.

A toxicologist from the Medical Examiner's Office took the stand and said that Kristin had had access to fentanyl, the drug that killed Greg, and that fifteen fentanyl patches had gone missing from the office. Amphetamines and meth were also missing.

The hospital had found a large amount of urine in Greg's bladder, indicating that he'd been semi-conscious or unconscious for six or more hours, yet Kristin had said that he'd spoken to her after 5 p.m.. There had been lividity in his lower body, suggesting that he might have been unconscious or dead for an hour to an hour and a half before the paramedics arrived. They had also discovered an unaccounted-for needle mark on Greg's arm, surrounded by a large bruise.

On 31st October, Kristin took the stand. She painted her childhood in rosy terms but started to cry when asked about her drug use and her flight to Mexico.

She said that Greg had fetched himself a drink of what she thought was water on the night before he died and that, the next morning, he'd been slurring his words. She'd called in sick for him and visited at lunchtime, then popped out to buy soup for them both. She'd bought a single rose at the same time. She and Greg had chatted as they ate the soup and she claimed that he'd admitted taking some of her prescription medication as he was upset.

Kristin continued with her version of events, stating that she'd gone back to work and spent most of the afternoon with Michael. After work, she'd returned home for a while before going shopping. On her return, she'd kissed Greg on the forehead then had a long bath, lasting almost an hour, and had done some work. When she next looked in on her husband he was cold and dead so she had called the emergency services.

When cross-examined, Kristin admitted telling a TV interviewer that Greg might have deliberately taken an overdose in order to frame her. She admitted keeping her drugs at work because Greg didn't trust her and often searched their house.

She said that she'd bought a yellow rose, surrounded by little flowers, on the day of her husband's death, planning to give it to her lover, Michael.

Guilty

The jury deliberated for only eight hours before finding her guilty, whereupon Kristin Rossum cried so hard that she came close to hyperventilating. She was sent to Las Colinas detention centre, where she continued to protest her innocence and vowed to appeal. On 12th December 2002, she was sentenced to life imprisonment without the possibility of parole. She was subsequently moved to Chowchilla Women's Prison in California.

Kristin became a janitor in the jail and then a cleaner, a far cry from her work as a toxicologist. By mid-2004, she was allowed to work in the prison yard.

Interview

In June 2009, I interviewed crime writer Caitlin Rother, who sat through almost all of Kristin Rossum's court appearances and subsequently wrote a book about the case, *Poisoned Love*.

So what does Caitlin think Kristin's motive was for killing her husband?

'I've never publicly stated whether I believed she was guilty or not,' says the Pulitzer-prize nominated journalist, 'but the prosecutor argued that she wanted to prevent her husband from telling her superiors at the San Diego County Medical Examiner's Office that she was having an affair with her boss, Michael Robertson, and also was doing methamphetamines again. As it turned out, she lost her beloved job, and her access to free meth in the lab was cut off, because they were both fired seven months before she was arrested. He went back to Australia before police were able to charge him, and she ultimately lost contact with him as well.'

Caitlin Rother has a degree in Psychology, so does she believe that Kristin was suffering from a personality disorder? 'To my knowledge, she was never diagnosed with one, but her personality traits and behaviours definitely fit the definition of a narcissist, which is common for killers.'

I then asked what Caitlin believed were Kristin's reasons for agreeing to give a television interview when her trial was pending. 'I think that she and her parents were hoping that *48 Hours*, which I think got the only interviews, would serve as an advocate for her and that such a show would generate sympathy for her in the public arena. The detective pointed out to me that if you watch closely when she cries, you don't see any tears.'

Caitlin contributed to a documentary about the Kristin Rossum case, *Women Who Kill*, which is frequently shown on American TV. She was able to bring her own understanding of addiction and substance abuse (an alcoholic relative committed suicide) to aid her understanding of Kristin's descent.

Kristin refused to meet Caitlin whilst the latter was researching the case but has she been in touch since? The investigative journalist says not. 'I don't think she'd ever tell me anything, although I guess she could conceivably say something after her federal appeal is exhausted. It may already be, but I have no way to check because I don't know if/where it was filed.' Caitlin doesn't believe that Kristin will ever admit her guilt: 'I'd say, not a chance.'

Asked for any final comments on what was a terrible waste of two young lives, Caitlin replied, 'Kristin had three relationships: one with her husband, whom she claimed to love but not be in love with; one with her married lover, Michael Robertson, with whom she was passionately in love and with whom she wanted to have children;

and one with methamphetamine. In the end, she chose the meth over the two living partners, and by doing so, cost Greg his life, cost herself her career, devastated two families, and ruined Michael Robertson's career.'

This medical technician insured his wife for a significant sum, after which she had a near-fatal accident followed by a fatal one...

An impoverished childhood

Bruce was born on 29th March 1955 to Huldah and Wiljo Moilanen in a small outpost called Mass City in Michigan. Huldah would later attest that her husband was an alcoholic, but others said that her viewpoint was tainted by bitterness at the couple's late divorce. Bruce was their fourth child and there was a fifteen-year gap between himself and his oldest brother. One of his brothers would later go to jail for sexually assaulting a child.

The family had very little money and were

regarded by many of the locals as slightly odd but Bruce had a talent for fixing cars and, after he left school, he took a course in auto-mechanics and worked in various car repair shops.

Medical training

Unsure which career path he wanted to take, Bruce went to Northern Michigan University in Marquette and trained as an emergency medical technician, but afterwards returned to car repair work, setting up his own business. He would often switch between one career and another, or even run two or three businesses at once.

Whilst skiing at a local resort, he met an excellent skier called Judy and they began dating. On 24th June 1978, they married. Judy was working at Marquette General Hospital as an administrative assistant and, by 1980, Bruce was working there too. He operated a mobile scanning machine, which he often took to a nearby hospital. Staff there assumed that he was single as he flirted outrageously and asked several of the nurses out.

Later, Bruce also set up a kennels, but he was seen to kick one dog and was very strict with the others. As a result, many of the locals were unwilling to board their animals with him.

A near-fatal accident

In autumn 1991, Judy and Bruce were doing some repairs on their home. Judy was standing on the patio and Bruce went up to the roof to do some work near the chimney. Seconds later, an 85 lb chimney block fell from the roof and hit Judy a glancing blow, the incident being witnessed by the couple's three-year-old daughter, Elise. Judy was concussed and had to be taken to the Emergency Room to have her head stitched, after which she spent four days in hospital. On her release, she had to wear a neck collar for several weeks. Medics agreed that, if she'd been standing slightly closer to the house, the blow would have proved fatal – the block had gone on to make a large hole in the patio.

An unexpected fire

Later that autumn, Judy and her daughter were asleep in the house when Bruce left to go hunting. She woke up to find smoke filling the rooms and found that he had carelessly dumped the smouldering ashes from the woodstove so that they set the woodpile on fire. Fortunately, she was able to extinguish the small fire before the basement caught alight.

Shortly afterwards, she confided in friends that she and Bruce were having marital problems and were going for counselling. He was in debt and they had to sell their vehicles in order to pay their bills.

A sudden death

On 29th November 1992, Judy, by now aged 35, took her dogs for a walk in the Michigan woods. One of the animals returned home without her and friends mounted a search; they found her body, shot through the chest. It seemed like a tragic hunting accident, but police were sceptical as Bruce showed no emotion when they broke the news to him and he remained emotionless when viewing the body of his dead wife. He explained this to them by saying that, as he worked in the operating room at the hospital, he saw dead bodies all the time. When asked where he had been on the afternoon when Judy was shot, he immediately listed lots of places and times.

Detectives became even more suspicious when they found out that Bruce would benefit to the tune of $330,000 under an 'accidental death' insurance clause. He had been taking out policies on his wife for some time.

They talked to his colleagues and supervisors

at the hospital and found out that he repeatedly showed up late for work and that he often absconded to a different part of the building to chat up various women. He claimed to be having an affair with one married woman but she wanted nothing to do with him.

Detectives also found out that Bruce Moilanen regularly filed insurance claims. Indeed, he had done so after Judy was hit by the chimney block as the block had damaged their patio. They examined his finances and found that neither his car repair business nor the kennels were in profit, and that he had several overdrafts.

They asked him to take a lie detector test but he said that he had to look after his little daughter and didn't have the time. Determined detectives arranged for him to have a polygraph at a later date but he cancelled again. He also cancelled further lie detector tests, explaining that he was on medication to help him sleep so his responses would be poor. In the same time frame, he wrote an inappropriate love letter to a married woman and suggested that he take her husband on a hunting trip: frightened for her own safety and that of her spouse, she contacted the police. Bruce had written that he was ready to get married again, yet Judy had only been dead for ten weeks...

In March, he handed in his notice at work. The hospital was relieved as he had been such a poor employee – one of the reasons that they'd kept him on was because his wife Judy had been such a wonderful worker. They told him not to work out his notice, that his resignation was effective immediately. At a loose end, Bruce began to declare his affection for various local women, all of whom regarded him as a somewhat frightening pest.

Lie detector

On 23rd April, Bruce finally took a polygraph test. Detectives also showed him one of the inappropriate letters he'd written to a married woman. To their surprise, his eyes filled with tears. They told him that they believed he'd shot his wife and asked if it was an accident or deliberate. 'I probably shouldn't say without an attorney,' Bruce replied. A few minutes later he confessed to shooting Judy, saying that she was going to leave him and take half of everything. He complained that she'd worked long hours and wasn't a good cook, that he'd had to take care of the house. His tone was self-pitying and he showed no remorse.

Bruce added that he'd bought the gun from a stranger, crept into the woods and shot his wife, then torched the firearm. He was taken to the local jail, where he attempted to hang himself with a sheet.

His daughter was handed over to relatives and, to their concern, she told them that Daddy had pushed a big brick onto Mummy. Court officials decided she was too young to testify, so she didn't have to take the stand.

Escape

A few days later, Bruce cleaned his cell and his door was unlocked for him to hand the jail's duty officer his bag of rubbish, but when the officer unlocked the door, Bruce threw pepper into his eyes and fled. He ran to a local park and was recaptured there twenty-five minutes later and returned to jail.

Meanwhile, detectives continued to look into the Moilanens' finances and found that Bruce had let his insurance policy lapse but had continued to pay for his wife's policy. He had also lied to them when he said that their daughter, Elise, was the beneficiary.

They put a chimney block on the edge of the roof and did the kind of roof repairs Bruce had done, watching to see if the block would dislodge. It didn't. Even when they jumped up and down, the block remained in place.

Bruce's trial, which lasted for eight days in December 1993, was virtually a foregone conclusion and, after slightly less than seven hours of deliberation, the jury found him guilty of first-degree premeditated murder. He showed no emotion. On 21st January 1994 he was sentenced to life without the possibility of parole.

26   Chante Mallard

Though she was a nurse's aide, Chante's behaviour was that of a sociopath when she hit a man with her car.

Daddy's girl

Chante was born on the 22nd June 1976 to Dorothy and James Mallard. The couple already had two sons and lived in Fort Worth, Texas. James worked for a truck firm whilst Dorothy was a housewife, and their lives revolved around the local Baptist Church. James doted on little Chante, a quiet child who showed a talent for music. By her teens, she was teaching Bible classes to younger children and, after graduation, she did a part-time nursing course.

At nineteen, Chante's parents helped her to

buy her first house but she got into debt and they agreed to bail her out. As she moved through her early- to mid-twenties, she became more of a party girl. She used drugs on a regular basis and increasingly had a problem with substance abuse.

An appalling act

On 26th October 2001, the 25-year-old nursing home attendant drove home after a night out during which she had taken Ecstasy, smoked marijuana and drunk alcohol with friends at a Fort Worth nightclub. She hit 37-year-old Gregory Biggs and he catapulted partway through her windscreen and stuck there. Chante had enough medical knowledge to save him but instead she drove home, with the former bricklayer still trapped inside her vehicle, moaning and begging for help.

Chante parked in her garage and left the conscious man in considerable pain. She later said that she looked in on him several times and apologised as he pleaded for medical assistance – but, months later, she allegedly told a friend that she had gone into the house and had sex with her boyfriend. Her friends also alleged that she had boasted, 'I ran over a white man.' (Chante Mallard is black.)

Gregory died within hours of shock and loss of blood, after which the nurse's aide phoned two male friends and asked them to dispose of the body. They duly did so, dumping the blood-spattered victim in a local park. He was found with glass splinters in his face and one of his legs was nearly amputated, but medics ascertained that he would have lived if he'd been treated promptly. The case became a homicide, though detectives had no idea who the perpetrator was.

Meanwhile, Chante removed the car seats from her car and burnt one that was bloodstained, although she left the charred seat in her front garden. She also removed most of the interior from her car. She told friends that she had wrecked the vehicle but was scared to tell her father as he hadn't quite finished paying for it.

No one at Mariner Health, the nursing home where she worked, noticed any change in her demeanour. She was always smiling and was well liked both by co-workers and residents.

The months passed and then police received a tip about one of the men who had dumped the body. Their investigation led them to Chante Mallard and she told them about the events of that night, claiming that she wasn't a bad person, that she acted out of fear.

Trial

Her trial began on 23rd June 2003 and gained widespread media coverage. The public were understandably scathing of Chante's actions, pointing out that she had let a man die a horrible death rather than save him and serve a sentence for driving under the influence. Many of them were particularly alarmed that she'd been working in the healthcare field yet was showing the traits of a sociopath.

The defence alleged that their client had accidentally struck a man and had panicked and made the wrong choice. They argued that this didn't amount to murder but the prosecution pointed out that Chante's actions meant that medics weren't given the opportunity to save Gregory Biggs's life.

On 27th June, after deliberating for less than an hour, the jury returned with a guilty verdict and Chante was sentenced to fifty years in prison. She wept and apologised repeatedly to Gregory's son, Brandon, who made a victim impact statement in court, offering his forgiveness. The Religious Studies student was widely praised by other religious individuals and groups for his magnanimous gesture.

Two of Chante's friends were sentenced to nine and ten years respectively for disposing of Gregory's body. An independent company later made a TV movie about the case, with Stephen Rea in the role of the victim, called *Stuck*.

PART SIX

PAPER MASKS

The bogus doctor is every patient's worst nightmare, especially when they are undergoing surgery in a private clinic, away from genuine healthcare professionals. Dr John Brown operated on patients in dirty garages and in the basement of his house. Only when carrying out surgical procedures did he feel free of his demons, so he was motivated to continue even when the authorities made strenuous efforts to close him down. Dean Faiello was a beautician yet he injected his patients with a local anaesthetic, in one instance fatally, whilst trying to improve his finances. In contrast, John Christie's lust drove him to pretend to be a doctor, and he subdued his patients with gas before sexually assaulting and murdering them.

27 John Brown

This GP failed his plastic surgery exams but decided to practise surgery regardless, with ultimately fatal results.

A strict childhood

John Ronald Brown was born into a strict Mormon family on 4th July 1922 and followed his physician father into the medical field, graduating from the University of Utah in 1947. For thirteen years he worked as a GP in California before deciding to train as a plastic surgeon. He sailed through the written exams but went to pieces during the oral assessment as authority figures reminded him of his father, whom he deeply feared.

A normal man would have said *Que sera, sera* and returned to his GP practice, but John decided to go ahead and perform surgery anyway, driven by an almost pathological desire to operate. He found his patients in the transgender community, taking on distraught males who had been turned down as unsuitable candidates by legitimate surgeons. Word soon got around that some of his patients fared better than others, but he was inexpensive and a last resort so he always had a waiting list.

John carried out sex reassignment surgery in his workplace rather than in a fully equipped hospital and lacked the back-up staff a hospital could provide. He couldn't match professional hygiene standards, and, when a patient almost died of a subsequent infection, his medical licence was revoked. He had now lost the right to work as a GP.

The bogus surgeon's first marriage failed when his wife ran off with his best friend. He remarried but his second wife died of cancer. In 1981, he married for a third time, going through an arranged marriage in the Caribbean. He was fifty-nine but his wife, who did not speak English, was only seventeen. The former doctor taught her his language and how to read and write, and they had two sons together. He was a good husband and a loving father, but he was still determined to operate on as many people as possible, even if his makeshift surgery was dirty and unkempt.

John attempted to practise medicine in various American states but he was barred, in time, from each of them. By the 1980s he was living in San Diego but working in Mexico, performing surgery on males in which he removed most of the penis but fashioned the remainder into a clitoris. Some were delighted with their new genitalia, whereas others were left disfigured, suffering from severe infections and in constant pain. One woman had to wear nappies for the rest of her life after he punctured her rectum, causing faeces to leak into her vagina on a daily basis. She eventually died in agony. Word of his failures spread, and the transgender community nicknamed him Butcher Brown.

By the late 1980s he was offering penis enlargements to heterosexual males and agreed to let a television company make a film about his operative techniques. They were perturbed to hear his patients screaming as the anaesthetic wore off during surgery, but John reassured them that this was normal and nothing to worry about. The FBI weren't convinced and, in 1990, he was sentenced to three years in prison for practising medicine illegally. His wife now divorced him, aware that he was incapable of changing.

Released after a year and a half, the maverick became a taxi driver. Sadly, by 1993 the lure of surgery became too great and he started operating again. He would operate in basement rooms and in garages, often using medically unqualified former patients as his assistants – they paid retrospectively for their operations by working for him.

By now, the former doctor was suffering from acute depression and told acquaintances that he was haunted by demons. He added that he only felt sane whilst carrying out surgery.

A murder charge

In 1998, John Brown was contacted by 79-year-old Philip Bondy from New York, who had an amputee fetish and wanted to have a leg removed. No reputable surgeon would have agreed to remove the healthy limb, but John promised to carry out the operation. John had previously arranged to amputate the left leg of one of Mr Bondy's friends, but the friend had sensibly backed out when the surgeon murmured something about buying a saw. By now the former doctor was both living and working in Tijuana, Mexico, in the hope of evading the authorities.

Philip Bondy travelled to San Diego on 7th May and Dr Brown met him at the airport. Shortly afterwards, he performed the surgery, stitched a flap of skin back over the cut surface and applied bandages, but the clock was ticking:

he had stretched the flap too tightly over the bone, causing the tissue to die. The wound became gangrenous and Mr Bondy, who had been driven back to his hotel room and left to convalesce in bed, endured an agonising death. John had, as usual, been totally fixated on the operation and had failed to offer any kind of post-operative care.

John Brown was consequently prosecuted in California for second-degree murder. The jury returned with a unanimous guilty verdict and he was sentenced to fifteen years to life.

Unremorseful, John said that God wanted him to take care of people, and that he planned to work on a cure for cancer from his prison cell. He will be ninety-one before he is released and possibly too frail to wield a surgical knife.

28 Dean Faiello

Greed motivated this beautician to pretend that he had the qualifications to carry out cosmetic surgery, with fatal results...

A difficult start

Dean Faiello was born on the 31st August 1959 to Carmel and Sam Faiello in New Jersey. Three years later the couple had a baby girl. Carmel was a loving stay-at-home mother but Sam was often abusive and the Faiellos separated when Dean was twelve.

Although his father often called him stupid, Dean did well at school and was voted Most Likely to Succeed. With his olive complexion and dark good looks he was very attractive to girls, though it soon became obvious he preferred boys.

He graduated from school and began to study engineering at a New York college but, without his mother's encouragement, he fell behind in his studies and soon dropped out. He began to drift from one job to another, finding his main enjoyment from partying in the gay scene.

Dean didn't develop a strong personality, perhaps because he simply didn't have to: men, women and transsexuals fell heavily for his face and lithe figure and were desperate to spend time in his company. He was also an excellent dancer who sometimes danced professionally at go-go bars.

HIV positive

By the mid-Eighties, Dean was HIV positive. Perhaps realising that he had to take responsibility for his life, he began to take work more seriously, setting up a small construction company and buying a run-down mansion house. However, he soon turned the place into Party Central and was often drunk or high on cocaine.

Fortunately, he entered into an exclusive relationship with a more stable man – also HIV positive – who ran a beauty salon. His new lover encouraged him to train as an electrologist – removing excess hair from men and women

– after which Dean went on to learn laser hair removal and built up a substantial client list.

Unfortunately the good times were about to end as his lover died of Aids in November 1995, after which Dean consoled himself by getting drunk and returning to heavy cocaine use. He moved his electrology business into a room in a medical practice and began to abuse a prescription nasal spray that contained opiates, telling a friend that he was only truly happy whilst taking drugs.

Later, he set up a new business in a medical complex close to Park Avenue, offering laser hair removal. His calm manner and the surgical whites he wore convinced everyone that he was a qualified doctor, and he told patients with skin problems that he was a dermatologist. He began to remove brown marks with laser technology, despite the fact that he didn't know the difference between a benign lesion and a cancerous one.

Desperate to increase his drug use, Dean stole a prescription pad from a doctor and forged her name. The forgery was discovered and, in October 1998, he was arrested. His father posted bail. The beautician pleaded guilty the following month and was sentenced to three years' probation plus a spell on a drug rehabilitation programme. It should have been a second chance, but he continued to offer laser removal of lesions – a job for a licensed physician rather than a cosmetologist – and, unknown to him, the medical authorities began to investigate.

Dean's life became even more complicated when his beloved mother died of cancer in August the following year. He now drank even more heavily than he had before and soon spent his inheritance, then maxed out on credit card after credit card. He also had to pay over $3,000 to a patient who took him to court, claiming that the hair removal on his back hadn't worked.

A downward path

The beautician was so broke that he had to rent out his palatial apartment and move into cheaper premises. By now he was openly lying to his patients, telling them that he'd graduated from medical school.

In October 2002 he was arraigned for badly scarring a patient whom he'd removed a tattoo from. Bailed by a friend, he went straight back to work. He also arranged to sell his house as, by now, he was half a million dollars in debt. Dean had always procured drugs through his more sophisticated club contacts but now he was reduced to buying from dealers on the street and, by 2003, was forced to put his house on the market in the hope of paying off some of his creditors.

When he was charged with deception, Dean admitted that he'd been falsely referring to himself as Dr Faiello. Yet, out on bail, he treated 35-year-old Maria Pilar Cruz, who suffered from black hairy tongue syndrome and had to have the hairs scraped off at the doctor's office, a procedure that caused her pain. She had found Dean via the Internet and was initially impressed by his professionalism as he injected her tongue with a local anaesthetic before painlessly removing the hairs via laser surgery.

However, Maria felt ill after her first visit and phoned Dean to complain of dizziness and sickness. To a physician, these were warning signs that she was reacting badly to the medication, but Dean told her that it was nothing to worry about, to just take an over-the-counter antidote.

Manslaughter

On the evening of 13th April 2003, he welcomed Maria back to his office – really just a room in a friend's apartment. Maria had been to Mass that morning and was in good spirits. At the doctor's urging, she paid cash.

As with her previous visit, Dean injected lidocaine into her tongue to anaesthetise the area.

Maria flushed heavily, a sign that she'd reacted badly to the medicine, but Dean either didn't notice her change of colour or didn't know that it meant she was in serious danger. As he got ready to start the procedure, Maria lost consciousness and began to fit.

The charlatan phoned a friend, who urged him to call an ambulance, but Dean knew that this would result in his arrest. Instead, he did nothing and, at some stage, Maria died. He then decided to conceal the death. Folding her body into a suitcase (she was a small, slender woman) he drove it to his former home and mixed up a big batch of concrete, using some to make a platform in the garage's storage cupboard before setting down the suitcase with its grisly cargo and pouring more concrete on top of it.

Maria's co-workers were alarmed when she didn't show up for work or phone in sick so they visited her apartment and found that her mail and newspapers were piling up. They, and her relatives, reported her missing and police began to investigate.

Shortly afterwards, the house sale went through and Dean moved in with another friend. It looked like he had literally got away with murder, although he was getting closer to his court date of 5th September, when he'd be sentenced for practising medicine without a licence.

The fugitive

Dean fretted about going to jail and decided that he couldn't face it. Instead, he jetted off to Costa Rica, living off the money he'd made from the sale of his house. Callous as ever, he let down the friend who had trustingly posted his bail.

The net was closing in, however, as detectives had accessed Maria's email account and found that she'd gone to see someone calling himself Dr Faiello on 13th April. Indeed, he was apparently the last person to see her alive. They visited the house he'd sold and saw the odd concrete structure. Breaking it open, they found Maria Cruz's corpse.

Dean was arrested at a hotel and at first fought extradition, but his health deteriorated in the Costa Rican jail as HIV-inhibiting medication wasn't freely available. He returned to New York where he decided to plead guilty to avoid going to trial. In 2005, he was sentenced to twenty years. He spends his days reading and doing crossword puzzles and has gained a significant amount of weight.

A similar case

Sadly, others have failed to learn from Dean Faiello's mistakes. Luiz Carlos Ribeiro had qualified as a doctor in his native Brazil but did not have a licence to practise medicine in the United States. Unfortunately he did so regardless of the law, performing cosmetic surgery on Brazilian immigrants.

Dr Ribeiro's operating theatre was the basement of a house in Framingham, Massachusetts, and instead of a surgical bed he had a massage couch. To cut costs, he didn't employ a qualified professional to monitor his patients' vital signs.

On 27th July 2006, he operated on 24-year-old Fabiola DePaula, reshaping her nose. She went back three days later for liposuction and this time the procedure went horribly wrong. There were complications and fat travelled to her lungs, causing a pulmonary embolism, whereupon she lost consciousness. Her friend rushed her to hospital in a car and doctors worked on her for twenty minutes but she died.

Dr Ribeiro, by now aged 51, was sentenced to two-and-a-half to three years in prison, after which he would face deportation. The woman who owned the house where he carried out the illegal procedures was charged with being an accessory and deported, whilst Dr Ribeiro's wife, who had acted as his assistant, was sentenced to one year.

29　John Christie

British true crime aficionados will probably remember John Christie, of 10 Rillington Place fame, for his failure to tell the authorities that Timothy Evans was innocent of the murders that he was subsequently hanged for. So great – and understandable – was the outcry at this miscarriage of justice that the fact that he pretended to be a qualified medic in order to subdue his victims has been largely forgotten over time.

A miserable childhood

John Reginald Christie, who later became known by his middle name of Reggie, was born on the 8th April 1898 to a passive mother and a strict disciplinarian of a father. He was terrified of the latter, who beat him for such supposed infractions as eating a tomato without permission and rocking backwards and forwards on a park bench. His father, a carpet designer who was also First Superintendent of the St John Ambulance Brigade, became increasingly irate with the frail boy and bestowed his favours on his other six children instead.

Reggie hated his older sisters as they bossed him around and he feared his grandparents, but was pleased when his mother's father died and he was able to view the old man in his coffin. He began to fantasise that everyone who ill-treated him would become similarly lifeless and he spent most of his spare time at the local graveyard. As a result of this, and his excessive hand-washing, the other children considered him odd.

The Christies were deeply religious and, outwardly, Reggie appeared equally puritanical, but he had the sexual desires of a growing boy – desires that he believed to be wrong. He was particularly perturbed when he looked at his sisters and felt lustful, particularly as he despised their dominant personalities. Love and hate were becoming entwined in his confused young mind.

At fifteen, he left school and became an assistant cinema operator, as he had a love of film and photography and an intrinsic understanding of machinery. He began dating a girl he met in church, but, when he attempted to have sex with her, he lost his erection. She told her friends and he became known, humiliatingly, in the locality as Reggie No Dick. At eighteen he joined the army but remained an outcast, taking his landlady's baby out in its pram whilst his comrades had fun in the pub. To outsiders, he was a shy youth with high colouring, the type of boy that you'd happily take home to mother, but inwardly he seethed with lust and rage.

Prostitutes

At nineteen, Reggie began to use prostitutes and may well have continued to do so when posted abroad to France. The young soldier was knocked unconscious by a shell and was so traumatised that afterwards he could only speak in a whisper. He would later exaggerate his injuries in order to get sympathy, telling acquaintances that he'd gone blind.

By the time he was twenty-one, he'd left the army and returned home to Halifax, where he began to date his neighbour, Ethel Waddington. They married the following year, though he struggled to consummate the marriage and often failed at subsequent attempts at intercourse. Soon he returned to prostitutes. However, he struggled to afford his regular visits to call girls from his mill worker's salary so retrained as a postman. Unable to resist temptation, he stole money orders from his mail sack, was caught and sentenced to seven months in prison.

Separated

The next few years saw Reggie become increasingly embroiled in crime. He left his wife with relatives in Sheffield and moved to London, ostensibly to make his fortune. But, in 1924, he was sent back to prison for two counts of larceny. On his release, he set up home with a prostitute, living off immoral earnings but, in 1929, he attacked her brutally with a cricket bat and was sentenced to six months' hard labour. In 1933, he went back to jail for stealing a car from a priest who had befriended him.

At this point, Reggie wrote to his wife from prison and suggested that they make a fresh start. By now, she hadn't seen him for nine years and she was bored and lonely, so acquiesced. The couple set up home in London but it was soon clear that marriage wasn't helping Reggie to cope with life and he spent many hours at his doctor's surgery, complaining of numerous imaginary ailments. His sympathetic GP prescribed sedatives and sleeping pills.

In December 1938, Reggie and Ethel Christie moved to 10 Rillington Place in London's Notting Hill. Though the end-of-terrace had three floors, it was very small. The Christies had the basement flat, the first floor housed an elderly gentleman and the top floor was unoccupied when the couple arrived.

Reggie joined the War Reserve Police as a special constable (they didn't check to see if he had a criminal record) and completed two first aid courses. Later he would pretend to have superior medical training...

The first known murder

Whilst working as a policeman, Christie befriended a young nurse called Ruth Fuerst who supplemented her income by selling sexual favours. In the same time frame, he was beaten up by a soldier for trying to have sex with the man's wife. Christie hated being a victim and was determined to take his rage out on someone, but he feared other men and their anger so decided to vent his wrath on the unsuspecting Ruth.

In August 1943, she accompanied him back to Rillington Place (Christie's biographer, Ludovic Kennedy, claimed that the killer had probably used his policeman status, threatening to report her if she didn't submit to him), where he strangled her on the bed, causing her to defecate and urinate. Undaunted, he stripped the bed and had sex with her corpse.

That same day, a telegram arrived from his wife to say that she was returning from visiting relatives and would be home that evening, so the killer put Ruth's corpse under the floorboards. He subsequently buried her in the garden rockery and would later admit that he never thought about her again.

The paper mask

John Reginald Christie now found himself attracted to 39-year-old Muriel Eady, who worked alongside him at an electronics firm. He knew that she would never sleep with him so pretended that he had a medical background and could cure her catarrh.

Muriel trustingly arrived at 10 Rillington Place one morning in October 1944 (she had previously socialised with Ethel Christie so had no reason to doubt Reggie's motives) and he held an inhalation device over her mouth and nose. At first, she was just inhaling Friar's Balsam, but when he released a bulldog clip on the tube, she also began to inhale gas that was coming from the gas point. As she lost consciousness, he strangled her and had sex with her still-warm body – he was able to spend a lot of time with it as his unsuspecting wife was again away visiting relatives in Sheffield. He buried Muriel's body in the garden, close to the previously buried corpse.

Reggie now began to encourage neighbours and acquaintances to call him 'the doc' and was always keen to suggest solutions for their minor health problems. As a middle-class man living in a working-class area, it was easy for him to sound knowledgeable and he told them that he'd had medical training in the army and the police.

The abortionist

In March 1948, new neighbours moved into the upstairs flat: Timothy and Beryl Evans. Timothy was a 25-year-old van driver who had the mental age of a ten-year-old and Beryl was expecting their first baby. She gave birth to a girl, Geraldine, and went back to work part-time, helped by her family and a babysitting friend.

In the autumn of 1949, Beryl confided in

Reggie 'the doc' Christie that she was pregnant again and had no idea how she'd cope. She'd have to give up her job and they'd never manage to pay the bills, plus, at nineteen, she wasn't ready to become a mother for the second time. Christie told her about his supposed years at medical school and offered to abort the foetus. Desperate, Beryl agreed.

Christie also showed Timothy his first aid certificates and said that, before the war, he had been training to be a doctor. He showed the illiterate Timothy his first aid manuals and the younger man looked at the pictures and was suitably impressed.

On Tuesday, 8th November, Timothy went to work and Ethel Christie went out for the day, after which Reggie ascended the stairs to the Evans's flat, carrying a piece of rubber tubing. She lay down on a quilt and he attached the tube to the gas pipe and put the tubing to her face. The teenager panicked and began to struggle, whereupon Reggie hit her about the head and strangled her with the rope he had secreted in his pocket. He subsequently had sex with her corpse. He was horrified when her babysitter came round and rattled the door handle, but the woman assumed that Beryl was angry with her for some reason and went away.

Reggie waited for Timothy Evans to come

home from work then showed him his wife's corpse, which was bleeding from the nose, mouth and genitals. He said that she had died during the abortion, and that he would now dispose of the corpse down the drain. Timothy, who had an IQ of 67 (as opposed to Reggie's 128) didn't ask for details of exactly how this disposal would be carried out.

The following night, Reggie told Timothy that he had given his baby, Geraldine, to a couple who wanted to adopt her. He coached Timothy to tell everyone that Beryl had taken the baby to visit her father in Brighton. In reality, Christie had strangled the little girl – she and her mother would later be found in the wash house of 10 Rillington Place.

The killer then persuaded Timothy to go and stay with relatives – but the young man missed his daughter so much that he returned to Rillington Place and asked to be put in touch with the couple who were supposedly caring for her. By now, Timothy's relatives were equally concerned about the child's disappearance, as they had telegraphed Beryl's father and the man had replied that Beryl hadn't visited him.

They questioned Timothy in depth about his wife and child and he couldn't supply them with a satisfactory answer, so they threatened to write to other relatives in an attempt to find out what was happening. Out of his depth, Timothy decided to go to the police. He determined to implicate himself as he was terrified of implicating Reggie, a former policeman, who had warned him that the police looked after their own kind.

Walking into Merthyr Vale Police Station, the police station closest to his family, he told the astonished desk detective, 'I have disposed of my wife.' When asked how, he said, 'Down the drains', the disposal method that Christie had told him he would use.

Asked to make a statement, Timothy said that a man in a cafe had sold him abortion pills, which he'd duly given to Beryl, but that she had died and he'd pushed her, head first, down the drain. He'd taken his baby to 'be looked after', then visited his relatives.

The police went to the drain at Rillington Place and found that they needed three strong men to lift the manhole cover – and that the drain was empty. They told Timothy this and he was deeply shocked, and made a subsequent statement implicating John Reginald Christie.

Reggie was brought in for questioning, but, as a former policeman and a man from a good family, he gave a much better account of himself than the bumbling Timothy. He dismissed his upstairs neighbour as a fantasist, something that others who knew Timothy had also told the police.

Detectives also questioned Ethel Christie but her husband had briefed her well and she told them that Beryl had gone elsewhere for an illegal abortion. They now searched the wash house and found the corpses of Beryl and little Geraldine. They told a stunned Timothy that they had found both bodies and arrested him for the murder of his wife and child. He was shocked to hear that Beryl had been strangled as this contrasted with the abortion story Reggie had fed him and which he'd believed completely. He was also absolutely devastated to hear that his baby, whom he had doted on, was dead.

Fitted up

Before long, the police were telling the media that Timothy Evans had confessed and they produced his supposed verbal statement, but, for a man who could neither read nor write, it contained the unlikely phrase 'She was incurring one debt after another' and referred to 'false pretences' and 'no fixed abode' – terms more frequently used by the police than by a man who was seven years old before he could even pronounce his own name. Timothy later told his mother that the police kept him awake until 5 a.m., badgering him to confess.

By that time, it's likely that the young man would have said anything in order to get some sleep. He apparently told detectives that he'd locked the wash house (it didn't have a lock) and that he'd strangled his baby, although he couldn't explain why. He'd carried her body and that of his wife to the wash house – an impossible task given that he was small in stature and only weighed ten stone, whilst his pregnant wife weighed nine. He had apparently moved the body down both flights of stairs without making a sound, as neither of the Christies awoke.

Later, when Timothy had rested, he said to his mother, 'I didn't do it, Mam. Christie done it. Ask him to come and see me. He's the only one who can help me now.'

Trial

On 11th January 1950, Timothy Evans' trial began at the Old Bailey. Reggie took the stand as the Crown's chief witness, describing the layout of the house and suggesting that Timothy was an angry young man who frequently rowed with Beryl. Whenever he was asked about something that might incriminate him, Reggie's voice faded to a near-whisper and, when he was urged to speak up, he said that his vocal cords had been damaged by gas poisoning in the war. This naturally assured him the sympathy of the court.

The defence suggested that Reggie had committed both murders but he denied this and talked at length about his health problems. Why, the jury doubtless wondered, would a sick man with chronic back pain want to murder a young woman and her baby? In contrast, Timothy was an unsympathetic figure, who apparently couldn't cope with domestic life.

Timothy claimed that Reggie had told him that Beryl died during the abortion, and that he had helped the older man to carry his wife's body to another flat in the building as the owner was in hospital. Reggie had volunteered to look after the baby the following day whilst Timothy was at work, and had subsequently told him that a couple in East Acton were fostering the child. His relatives had later questioned him about the whereabouts of his wife and daughter, whereupon he'd gone to the police.

Timothy explained his confession to the double murder by saying that he feared the police would beat him up – one of the detectives had terrified him by playing the role of 'Bad Cop' during his interrogation. He also said that, having been doubly bereaved, he felt that he had nothing left to live for, so was indifferent to being hanged.

No one was surprised when the jury took only forty minutes to return with a unanimous guilty verdict and he was sentenced to death. Timothy was stunned – but Reggie, perhaps feeling guilty, burst into tears.

Guilt

In the days that followed, John Reginald Christie genuinely seemed to be distraught that an innocent man would die for his crimes. He stopped eating, lost weight and returned to his doctor's surgery, where he wept and complained that his nerves were bad. He was prescribed a stronger sedative and advised to have a holiday with his wife. He did so, and, on his return, was given a medical certificate for a month off work. Yet, despite his guilt, he did not go to the authorities and confess to the murders, so Timothy Evans was duly hanged.

For the next two years, the Christies remained at Rillington Place, though the house had a change of landlord. The new landlord was Jamaican and let the other rooms to black tenants, something that offended Reggie's racist sensibilities. His nerves worsened, his health declined further and he stopped attempting to have intercourse with his wife. His doctor sent him to see a psychiatrist, who concluded that he was a latent homosexual and deeply neurotic. He wanted to treat Reggie as an inpatient but the man declined.

A domestic murder

On 6th December 1952, the mild-mannered man, who had been working as a clerk, handed in his notice, saying that he had found a better job in Sheffield. Just over a week later, on the 14th, he strangled his wife with one of her own stockings as she slept. He left her there for three days, and then hid her under the floorboards of the front room, sprinkling floral disinfectant around the area every day.

Reggie now invented story after story to explain away his wife's disappearance. He told some people that she was visiting relatives, and told others that she was caring for her sister who had just had a gynaecological operation. He also showed them a telegram that Ethel had ostensibly sent.

Deep down, however, the killer, having given up work, was not waving but drowning and running out of cash. He sold his furniture in order to have money to live off and forged Ethel's signature so that he could raid her savings book. Then he went out to the pub, determined to meet a woman for sexual release.

A prostitute's murder

In mid-January, Reggie met up with 26-year-old streetwalker Kathleen Maloney. He'd previously taken photographs of one of her friends after persuading her to take off her clothes. Now he made some excuse to get Kathleen back to Rillington Place, where he put his medical apparatus over her face and gassed her. When she became drowsy, he strangled her and had sex with her corpse. Afterwards, he pulled away a large cupboard to reveal an alcove, put her body there and covered it with ashes, then slid the cupboard back into place.

The abortionist strikes again

That same month, Reggie met 25-year-old waitress Rita Nelson. The young woman was single, seven months pregnant and had recently left her native Belfast; she knew no one in London and was frightened of the impending birth and motherhood. Reggie told her that he was an abortionist and she accompanied him back to his flat, where he persuaded her to inhale gas. She broke free and struggled, but he strangled her and had necrophiliac sex before putting her body in the alcove next to Kathleen's corpse.

The one that got away

His medical ruse was working well, so the unemployed clerk continued to use it. He promised a woman he met in a cafe, Margaret Forrest, that he could cure her migraines by getting her to inhale a certain type of gas. He would make no charge for this and his wife would make her a nice cup of tea. When she questioned his qualifications, he said that he was a doctor who had been struck off for performing an illegal abortion but that he still enjoyed curing the sick. Margaret made two appointments for the treatment but failed to turn up, a move that undoubtedly saved her life.

The final murder victim

Reggie met his final victim, 26-year-old Hectorina MacLennan, in a cafe and found out that she was looking for a flat, but he was disappointed when she showed up with her boyfriend. He persuaded her to come back to the house alone and attempted to gas her but she rushed into the hall. Grabbing her, he choked her unconscious, murdered her and violated her corpse. Afterwards, he stowed her away in the alcove with the other bodies, using blankets and gags to soak up the liquids the corpses released.

By mid-March, as the temperature rose, the smell in the house became unpleasant and Reggie had substantial rent arrears. He knew that he had to get out of there. With his usual cunning, he managed to sub-let the flat, even though he had no right to do this. The new tenants gave him three months' rent in advance and Reggie disappeared into the night.

His landlord was annoyed to find out what he had done, moved the new tenants out and began to clean up the dilapidated building. Looking into the alcove, he saw a naked corpse and called the police. They investigated and found three bodies in the recess, Ethel Christie under the floorboards and two more female bodies in the garden, which had already been partially dug up by Reggie's dog.

When the newspapers broke the story, Reggie was staying in a men's hostel. He heard the news on the radio and fled, walking aimlessly around London, although he propositioned one pregnant young lady and told her he was a doctor. He spent his days in cafes and his nights sleeping rough. After a few days, a policeman recognised him, cold and hungry, leaning over the embankment near Putney Bridge. The officer spoke to him gently, and the killer seemed relieved that it was all over and agreed to accompany him to the nearest police station to make a statement. He later said that he was very well treated by the police.

Restored to health

Ironically, the serial killer blossomed in prison. He gained weight, slept well and became Brixton's chess champion. The doctors who had to interview him, however, found him to be a hypocrite with an air of bogus gentility. He said that he found masturbation disgusting and that he also hated pubs – yet he had gone to bars to pick up prostitutes.

He admitted to murdering seven women but said that the prostitutes had made passes at him and wouldn't take no for an answer, causing him to go berserk. In contrast, the respectable women – namely Mrs Evans, Mrs Eady and Mrs Christie – had died whilst he was trying to alleviate their suffering. (He said that his wife had begun to have convulsions after taking an overdose of barbiturates and that he'd strangled her to put her out of her misery.)

He refused to admit to killing baby Geraldine as this conflicted with his view of himself as a respectable man. Cleaning up the streets was one thing but murdering a fourteen-month-old child was something else. The doctors found that his facility for self-deception was unparalleled and that he was a pathological liar.

Reggie's trial opened at the Old Bailey on 22nd June 1953, almost four years after he had helped to condemn Timothy Evans. The defence said that he was suffering from an abnormality of mind and didn't know what he was doing, whilst the prosecution claimed that, although he was highly abnormal, he knew both what he was doing and that it was wrong. The judge agreed with the latter's appraisal and sentenced John Reginald Christie to death. On 15th January 1953, he was hanged.

PART SEVEN

UNBRIDLED LUST

John Reginald Christie, in the Paper Masks section, pretended to be a medic in order to subdue women and enjoy necrophiliac sex with them, but in the following instances, the men were qualified medics and paramedics who allegedly abused their positions of power. Most of these men had controlling personalities, often hidden behind a superficial charm. Ambulance driver Francis Fahey concealed his angry desires until he was alone with his vulnerable victims, whilst Dr Joseph Charalambous was willing to arrange for the contract killing of a teenage girl whom he had inappropriately kissed. Anthony Joyner was an outwardly friendly young man who sexually assaulted and killed the elderly women in his care and Dr Dubria was a respected medic who allegedly raped, and inadvertently took the life of, a female friend. Radiographer Bobby Joe Long was mild-mannered until he had his victims cornered, whereupon he became a vicious and relentless predator. A combination of nature and nurture had left him with a prodigious sex drive, coupled with a deadly rage.

30   Francis Fahey

Although this ambulance driver had mental health problems for years, it seems that he only became a bondage killer after he lost his job and built up massive debts.

Psychiatric problems

At first sight, Francis Michael Fahey was a very ordinary man – a slightly overweight ambulance driver and stretcher-bearer who lived in Queensland, Australia. In the early 1990s he married a woman with three daughters and initially seemed to cope with family life but, as time passed, he became increasingly moody and sometimes ferociously angry with his wife and stepdaughters. Over the next few years he spent time as an outpatient at various mental health facilities. He told psychiatrists that he'd often contemplated suicide.

Francis eventually pretended that he was incapacitated and claimed Au$88,000 in sick pay that he was not entitled to. When this was discovered, he was ordered to pay it back and sentenced to fifteen months in jail, but he only spent a week in prison before being bailed on appeal. He lost the appeal but the paperwork went missing so he wasn't returned to custody.

By early 2002, the 51-year-old ambulance driver had been dismissed from his job; he now had difficulty sleeping and showed clinical levels of depression. His mood swings also worsened. He told a psychiatrist that he had seen too much illness and death as a result of his ambulance work, but the psychiatrist wasn't convinced that this was the true reason for his malaise. Francis claimed that he had post-traumatic stress disorder and he took medication for this but it didn't seem to help.

Jasmin's murder

On 8th August 2002, Francis went out in his four-wheel-drive and picked up 41-year-old prostitute and drug addict Jasmin Crathern. He drove her to a quiet location, tied her up and stabbed her fourteen times with a bayonet. One stab wound to her back was delivered with such force that it went all the way through to her chest, whilst another knife wound pierced her throat. Afterwards, he dumped her partially clothed body in a vacant lot at Hendra in Brisbane before washing her blood from his body with bottles of mineral water and returning home to his wife and stepfamily.

The body was found the next day and immediately yielded clues as there was semen on Jasmin's black blouse and the earth around her body showed tyre tracks from a rare type of imported tyre.

Julie's murder

Francis relived the murder over and over and fantasised about what he would do the next time or so he would later tell the police. On 26th February 2003, he went out driving in the early hours of the morning and picked up prostitute Julie McColl. A drug addict who had hepatitis C, she looked older then her forty-two years.

The ambulance driver told her that he was looking for 'something different' and, when she asked for more details, said that he wanted to tie and blindfold her. She offered to tie *him* up but he explained that this wasn't his thing. Seeing her hesitate, the ambulance driver said that he was a happily married man with kids but had this one little kink that he didn't want to bother his wife with. When he offered Julie Au$500, she agreed to his demands. She had no idea that a bayonet, still bearing his first victim's dried blood, was lying under the driving seat.

Francis drove for ten miles to a picnic site at Deep Water Bend, a dark area in Brisbane. Unknown to him, two fishermen had seen his distinctive vehicle – and, at 3.30 a.m. they heard a woman scream.

Meanwhile, the lust-filled driver had stripped his victim naked and bound her feet and hands, circling the rope around her breasts and back. He also blindfolded her and gagged her with a strip of gauze. When she was lying trussed-up on her stomach and completely vulnerable, he stabbed her in the back and shoulders again and again. His blade pierced her body twenty-four times, and one wound to the breast pierced a major artery, after which she quickly bled to death. Dumping the body, he returned to family life.

The one that got away

Police appealed to the local prostitute community to tell them about any clients who had requested bondage, and 24-year-old Jacinda Horne came forward. She said that a man driving a four-wheel utility vehicle – she described it in impressive detail – had picked her up earlier on the night Julie died. She'd got into his vehicle and he'd said that his name was Mike (it was indeed his middle name) and had asked to bind and blindfold her. He'd been really persuasive and offered big money but she'd declined and hurriedly left the cab. Shortly afterwards, it seems that he'd picked up Julie, with fatal results.

Detectives studied CCTV footage taken in the red light district on that night and found the suspect vehicle, a Mitsubishi Trident. They used the vehicle registration to trace its owner, Francis Michael Fahey. At this point, the ambulance driver had no idea that he was under surveillance or that his arrest was imminent. Taking DNA from discarded cigarette ends in his cab, forensic experts matched it with the sperm found on Jasmin's blouse, proving that the man named after two saints was far from saintly. His tyres also matched the tyre marks found at the first murder scene.

Francis was visibly surprised when detectives arrested him on 7th May 2003, as he was sure he'd covered his tracks. At first he denied everything. His wife was also convinced they'd got the wrong man, but a search of their house turned up ropes similar to those used on Julie McColl, and dried blood on the bayonet proved to be from both victims. Shortly afterwards, the double murderer confessed, telling detectives, 'I've spent all my fucking life saving lives. Now I'm taking them and I don't know why.' He added that he was glad that he hadn't killed any of his own family. Psychiatrists thought that he probably had a puritanical attitude towards prostitution, that he saw himself as cleaning up the streets.

Trial

At his trial in 2006, the prosecution said that the first sexual murder had whetted Francis's appetite, that he'd put more planning into the second. The defence, in turn, tried to blame the couple's lodger, as he'd also had access to the four-wheel-drive, the murder vehicle.

The jury took just four hours to find the former ambulance driver, now aged fifty-three, guilty of both murders, and he was sentenced to twenty-five years. His wife said outside the court that his ambulance work had robbed him of his vitality and contributed to his psychiatric problems. She subsequently divorced him.

In 2006, Jacinda Horne, whose detailed account of Francis's vehicle had led to his being traced by police, was given a Au$100,000 reward by the Queensland government.

31　Dr Joseph Charalambous

Unhealthily drawn to under age girls – he often said he'd rather date two fifteen-year-olds than a thirty-year-old – this Canada-based GP had one of his teenage patients murdered to prevent her testifying against him.

Early influences

Josephakis was born on 5th April 1952 in Cyprus, the second child of Petrou and Eleodoros Charalambous. He was close to his mother but hated his father, a strict disciplinarian. The couple went on to have a third child, moving the family to Canada when Joseph (his name was soon shortened to this) was eight years old.

As a boy, he had a desperate need to control his environment and was full of nervous energy, understandable for someone growing up in an abusive household. Neighbours often heard screams coming from the house.

By his teens, Joseph was ashamed of his seamstress mother and watchmaker father; he wanted to enter the professional classes and decided to become a doctor. He did well at school and also studied karate in his spare time, determined to compensate for his slim build and small stature. The youth was determined to become a man as quickly as possible, to exert control, and he succeeded, becoming so good at martial arts that he was able to throw his drunken, womanising father out of the house.

Joseph went to medical school, where many of the other students found him to be arrogant and domineering. However, there was worse to come. In December 1977, he asked a woman out and she rebuffed him. Enraged, he punched her in the face and was so incensed that she feared for her life. He was taken to court the following summer and placed on probation for a year.

In January 1979, he got into an altercation over a prostitute and fired a warning shot from his rifle, slightly injuring a man's hand. Incredibly, he still wasn't expelled from the university. Nor was he penalised that summer when he paid a prostitute to fellate him in his car, then suddenly hit her about the head. She called the police, but they let her violent client go, reluctant to besmirch a promising medical career.

Joseph Charalambous graduated from the University of British Columbia in 1981 and began work as an intern. He had sacrificed much of his youth to study medicine, but, by adulthood, the sacrifice was paying off and the young doctor bought himself a house and later a surgery in Coquitlam. He earned a good salary but spent freely on the horses, poker and even the lottery, chalking up large debts. He'd sometimes stay at the casino all night and arrive at work looking worn-out.

Even after a tiring day, he didn't like to be alone, so taught karate in the evenings (he was a black belt) and sometimes brought his students back to party until the early hours.

Seduction

In 1984, Joseph hit his live-in girlfriend and she left him. Around about the same time, one of his childhood friends got back in touch and he beat and attempted to rape her. The traumatised woman called the police but Joseph managed to persuade them that she'd suffered a psychotic episode.

The following year, he became obsessed with

a fifteen-year-old patient called Shelley Joel. He originally counselled her after she was raped, but soon progressed to asking her out. He had sex with her whilst she was still a minor and, when she turned sixteen, she moved in with him despite the fact that he was twice her age.

Shelley's mother and stepfather protested, only to find that someone had set fire to their car. They continued to beg their daughter to leave the controlling doctor, whereupon someone poured acid over their other vehicle. By now, Joseph was beating Shelley and it was obvious that she was miserable and afraid. He also told her that he would kill her mother if the older woman continued to intervene.

Determined to free her impressionable daughter from the doctor's clutches, Shelley's mother, Jacqueline, filed a complaint, but Joseph persuaded Shelley to marry him, knowing that the medical school would look ridiculous if they barred him from medical practice for sleeping with the young woman who'd become his wife. Shortly after the wedding, the teenager became pregnant and, nine months later, gave birth to a baby girl.

Finally, college officials came back with their verdict and gave the doctor a hefty fine plus six months' suspension from duty. At the start of 1989, he was forced to remortgage his house yet still continued to lose large amounts of money on the horses. After his six-month suspension, he also continued to flirt inappropriately with his younger patients. By now, Shelley had given him a second child – a son – and he was finding her less desirable. He lusted after young, inexperienced flesh.

Another complaint

Joseph regularly behaved inappropriately, asking his female teenage patients about their sex lives. Young women who turned up with hay fever were surprised when the doctor insisted that they strip and undergo a full breast examination. There wasn't a nurse present during these intimate examinations.

Two years after his suspension period ended, Joseph kissed two of his teenage patients, sisters Katie and Sian Simmonds, on the lips and phoned them later to ask how they were. Concerned, the girls told their father and he put in a formal complaint to the British Columbia College of Physicians and Surgeons. Later, the doctor phoned them and tried to persuade them to drop the charges. They refused.

The doctor told Shelley that the only way to silence them would be to kill them. He also talked about murdering the entire panel. Shelley, who had by now given her husband a third child, another girl, said little, terrified of enraging him further and of receiving another beating at his hands. Remembering that he'd threatened to kill her mother, she didn't take these new threats seriously.

Chillingly, Joseph began to drive past the apartment where the girls lived, checking up on their movements. In early 1993, he persuaded David Schlender, a biker with a drug problem whom he knew through his karate class, to kill one of the girls. The man had previously left a drug dealer for dead and was badly in need of money. The deal was arranged through an intermediary, Brian West.

David knew that the girls had a red jeep so he deliberately ran his keys along the paintwork to create a long, deep scratch, then knocked on the downstairs door and asked the woman who answered if she owned the vehicle, explaining that he'd accidentally damaged it. She said no, that it belonged to the girls upstairs. David then knocked on the Simmonds's door and told Sian the same story. She hurried out to her vehicle and became visibly upset, but David got her to go back into the house by asking to use the bathroom whilst she looked over his insurance documents.

Moments later, he shot her in the jaw with a Ruger pistol, fitted with a home-made silencer.

She backed away and he shot her again, the bullet entering her arm. This time Sian – a day short of her twentieth birthday – lunged at him and tried to grab the gun. Panicking, the hired killer battered her with the weapon. She collapsed, but he continued to strike her another six times. The killer fled, leaving his insurance papers behind. His ungainly flight was spotted by the postman, and shortly afterwards, the teenager's corpse was found by her aunt.

Confession

Brought in for questioning, David Schlender confessed, although he blamed the murder on Sian, saying that he wouldn't have shot her if she hadn't started screaming. He implicated fellow biker Brian West, who had given him the gun and silencer.

Meanwhile, Sian's family fled the area, terrified that they would be murdered next. They had their suspicions that Dr Charalambous was behind Sian's death and said so to police. In turn, detectives bugged the doctor's home. They were perturbed to hear him tell Shelley that he might be returning to Cyprus and were even more alarmed when they heard him beating Shelley up.

Soon Shelley began an affair with a policeman

and left the doctor, taking her three children with her. Now, she was willing to speak openly about her husband's threats to murder various people who had crossed him, and she told the police everything she knew about the medic's schemes. On 28th May 1993, detectives arrested both Dr Charalambous and Brian West.

Trial

Four months after Sian's murder, David Schlender was sentenced to life imprisonment. He was also given fifteen years for the earlier attempted murder of a drug dealer. He later gave a further statement to police, saying that Brian West might have been given C$50,000 by Dr Joseph Charalambous to arrange Sian's death.

In custody, the doctor opted for a judge-only trial. The proceedings finally began on 24th October 1994 and he pleaded not guilty from behind bulletproof glass.

David Schlender took the stand and said that he'd never seen the doctor before, that Brian West had organised the murder. Katie Simmonds then testified that she and her sister had complained about Joseph in September 1991 and that he'd subsequently phoned them, trying to get them to retract their statements.

Shelley, the doctor's wife, also testified against him. Now in the Witness Protection Program, she told of how often her husband had spoken about killing the Simmonds sisters. She also said that he had gone to great lengths to track down Brian West. Later, the doctor had told her about how the murder was carried out and, thereafter, she had feared for her own safety. She was now divorcing him.

The doctor himself took the stand and admitted driving past the Simmonds's house but said that he was just trying to get up the nerve to talk to their father. He'd sent Brian West to talk them out of pressing charges, knowing that the biker looked intimidating. He said that he'd visited Brian after the murder because he wondered if the man had anything to do with Sian's death. Brian had allegedly admitted to knowing David Schlender and he, Joseph, had been shocked at this. Brian had then told him that David had gone over to the sisters' flat to scare them but had ended up murdering one of them by mistake.

On 29th November 1994, Judge McKinnon delivered his verdict: guilty. The spectators, most of whom had loved his innocent victim, burst into applause. The following month, Dr Joseph Charalambous was barred from practising medicine and was sent to a federal penitentiary to begin his life sentence. For the first few weeks he felt depressed but then he began to exercise and his mood improved.

When he had exhausted the appeals process, he unsuccessfully requested a new trial, claiming that Shelley's affair with a police officer had played a part in her testifying against him. In 2006, he gave an interview to the *Vancouver Sun,* in which he again proclaimed his innocence.

32   Anthony Joyner

This young man was comparatively unusual in that the targets of his lust were elderly women.

A soft-spoken young man

In 1982, the Kearsley Home of Christ Church Hospital in Pennsylvania, which had become a retirement home, interviewed candidates for the post of diet technician. One candidate, 22-year-old Anthony Joyner, was especially impressive, polite to both interviewers and residents, chatting easily to the elderly ladies who had made Kearsley their final abode. Although his slight build meant that his friends jokingly called him a faggot, he did in fact have a girlfriend.

Anthony soon became a familiar sight at Kearsley, ascertaining the residents' nutritional needs and spending time with them at barbecues and cream teas. He was a hard worker and well liked by his colleagues and by many of the older women, with whom he had a special rapport. The building had been made into sixty apartments so that each resident had their privacy as well as access to a communal lounge, an on-site doctor and private hospital facilities. There was also a security guard.

An unexpected death

One of the home's oldest residents, 92-year-old Margaret Eckard was also the most lively, so a nurse was surprised to find her lying dead on the floor on the morning of 21st January 1983. There was bruising around her nose and mouth alongside smears of blood. Further examination revealed traces of blood in her vagina and anus, but dead bodies sometimes leak bloody fluid so the doctor decided that she had died of natural causes and she was duly buried.

Another unexpected death

The following month, on the 12th February, 85-year-old Katherine Maxwell's door was found to be open, and when a nurse peaked in, she saw the octogenarian lying dead on top of the bed. Her pyjamas were streaked with blood. Again, the death was put down to natural causes and no autopsy was performed.

Suspicion grows

Shortly afterwards, 86-year-old Elizabeth Monroe was found dead in her bed. Again, there was bleeding from the vagina. The home's usual physician, Dr Williams, was out on call, so another physician did the paperwork, reporting that Elizabeth had died of natural causes. When Dr Williams returned and heard that a third resident had died with blood smears in the genital area, he asked for an autopsy but the body had already been embalmed. The medical examiner assured him that there was nothing to worry about, that his patient had died of illness associated with old age.

The death toll mounts

Lillie Amlie, 89, was the next unexpected death. Despite her advancing years, she had a boyfriend and loved to party. She had been in her usual high spirits on 1st June 1983, had gone for a late-afternoon nap, but then failed to arrive in the dining room for her evening meal. A nurse investigated and found her face down in the bath, which only had a few inches of lukewarm water in it. Strangely, she was wearing stockings and jewellery and there was blood around her nose, mouth, vagina and anus. However, Lillie had had a heart condition and the staff decided that she must have slipped and fallen into the tub.

Two more horrible deaths

Eugenia Borda, 90, a religious woman who was believed to have been a virgin, was the next to be found dead in her bed. There was blood around her nose, mouth, vagina and anus. Dr Williams was so alarmed at this pattern – convinced by now that it indicated rape – that he refused to sign the death certificate.

A few hours later, 72-year-old Mildred Alston was found dead across the hall, her panties lying next to the bed. She too had blood around her face and genitals. The medical examiner ruled that both women had been murdered, Eugenia of strangulation and Mildred of suffocation.

Detectives investigated and found that

Mildred's wedding and engagement rings and her purse had been stolen. Security was good so they suspected an inside job.

They began to question the friends and family of every employee and struck gold when one said that Anthony Joyner had boasted of raping women to prove that he was a man.

Taken into custody, Anthony soon broke down and admitted, 'I killed all of them.' He said that he'd done so after fights with his girlfriend, but he played down the murder element, saying that he'd put pillows over the sleeping women's heads so that they wouldn't recognise him as he raped them and that they'd accidentally died of suffocation during the sexual assaults. In another instance, he'd stuffed a rag into a victim's mouth to stop her screaming and she'd choked to death on the rag.

He talked on, admitting that he'd mainly entered the building at night through the cellar and sneaked into the residents' rooms. He'd chosen most of his victims at random, with the exception of Mrs Amlie, who had confronted him when he stole $20 from her. Disturbingly, he had responded by telling her how attractive she was. He had sneaked into her apartment again one afternoon, planning to steal further cash, only to find her about to take a bath, whereupon he'd thrown her onto the bed, raped her and held a pillow over her face. Believing that she was dead, he'd gone to loot through her apartment but she'd revived and tried to leave the room. Grabbing her, he'd dragged her to the bathroom and held her down in the bath until she drowned.

Trial

Anthony was sent to a Philadelphia detention centre, where he was denied bail. He soon started to rewrite history, accusing detectives of framing him, but the autopsies showed that all six women had been raped and murdered and Anthony had no alibi. He had also admitted previously breaking into an apartment and raping a 62-year-old woman some time before starting the Kearsley job.

At his trial in April 1984, Anthony's ex-girlfriend testified against him, saying that he'd told her he would soon be famous. He had also allegedly told her that there had been lots of murders at the home.

The diet technician took the stand and said that he'd been pushed around by detectives and that they had sworn at him despite the fact that he never used bad language. Facing the death penalty, he was fighting for his life.

The jury were out for ten hours then found him guilty of all six murders, although they were deadlocked over the penalty. It was the judge who imposed a sentence of life imprisonment. Anthony smiled when he heard this, relieved to avoid execution.

33   Dr Samson Dubria

Although this resident physician has always protested his innocence, he was convicted of murder, the alleged motive being lust.

A model student

Samson (which was soon shortened to Sam) Dubria was born in 1963 to Pat and Lourdes Dubria in Glendale, California. A bright child, he went on to study at Rochester University in New York and the University of California before attending the George Washington School of Medicine.

By 1990, Sam was resident physician at a veterans hospital in New Jersey. Many of the nurses were attracted to his oriental good looks but he fell for Jennifer Klapper, who worked in the medical library. The beautiful young librarian explained to him that she had a boyfriend so only wanted a platonic relationship. The doctor readily agreed to this and often met the twenty-year-old for drinks after work.

In the summer of 1991, Sam asked her to accompany him on holiday but Jennifer wasn't sure if this was a good idea and asked her parents for their input. They said that she was a sensible young woman and that she should trust her judgement, so Jennifer decided to go.

Sam drove her to meet his parents, who lived near Los Angeles, and they stayed overnight then drove on to an inn near San Diego. During the holiday, Jennifer made a lengthy, loving phone call to her boyfriend, a call that her friend Sam was aware of. Later, the prosecution and defence would have very different views of what happened on that fateful night of 16th August 1991.

The first that the authorities knew of any problem was when they received a call from the doctor, stating that his girlfriend had died suddenly. Paramedics arrived to find him desperately doing CPR but it was already too late. Sam said that he and Jennifer had enjoyed a sex session and that, shortly afterwards, she had collapsed.

Jennifer's body was autopsied by Dr Leona Jariwala. She noted that the girl's ski-pants were inside out, there was semen in her body and some marks on her face. Subsequent toxicology tests showed traces of chloroform. Determined to get a second opinion, the doctor sent further bodily samples to an independent laboratory and they too confirmed the results – that Jennifer had died of chloroform poisoning.

When detectives confronted the doctor, he said that he believed he'd driven to California behind a chemical lorry that contained chloroform. He said he'd felt dizzy during the drive.

In March 1992, Sam Dubria was arrested and stood trial for Jennifer's murder. The prosecution alleged that he had chloroformed her in order to rape her, and that she had died accidentally during the sexual assault. The defence said that the 28-year-old doctor had had consensual sex with Miss Klapper, and that her death was a tragic accident.

In 1993, the doctor – still protesting his innocence – was sentenced to life imprisonment. His family immediately began a campaign to have him released. In the summer of 2007, his attorneys asked for his conviction to be set aside, stating that Jennifer Klapper had previously made hospital visits complaining of a rapid heartbeat – information that had been withheld from the court. They also stated that the chloroform allegedly found in samples from her body could have come about through contamination in the laboratory.

A similar case

Britain witnessed a spate of drugged rapes by a male nurse in the late 1990s, which ultimately led to a murder charge. Kevin Cobb, who worked in the casualty unit of St Peter's Hospital in Chertsey, Surrey, injected several female patients with midazolam, a tranquilliser that causes short-term memory loss. When they were unconscious, he raped them, often striking late at night when the hospital was quiet.

He was friends with another nurse, Susan Annis, whom he secretly lusted after. One day, when they were on a residential nursing course together, he slipped a date rape drug into her drink. He accompanied her back to her room and raped her after she lost consciousness – but Susan had a bad reaction to the drug and died. Kevin told his fellow nurses that he'd desperately performed CPR but had been unable to save her; the 31-year-old woman was found to have a minor heart complaint and her sudden death was attributed to this. Kevin wept copiously at her funeral and everyone felt sorry for the man.

Unfortunately his friend's demise wasn't enough for him to stop his criminal acts and he raped another patient, who woke up during the sexual assault and was able to notify the authorities. They found midazolam in her system and Kevin was swiftly arrested. Traces of the drug were found in his pockets, and two other women came forward to make rape allegations against him, although he continued to protest his innocence.

In May 2000, the 38-year-old was convicted of manslaughter, two rapes and four counts of administering drugs with intent to rape. He was given seven life sentences. Police later said that they were convinced he had raped other patients but that the drug had impaired their memory of events.

34   Bobby Joe Long

Halfway through his murder spree, this serial killer began work as an X-ray technician in a Florida hospital. Some of his patients were outraged when he touched them inappropriately, but the sexually insatiable Bobby Joe was capable of much, much worse.

Early confusion

Bobby Joe Long was born on the 14th October 1953 in Kenova, West Virginia, to Louella and Joe Long; she was seventeen, he twenty-three. Within a year of their marriage, Louella had given birth to Bobby Joe, but the marriage swiftly deteriorated and, by 1955, the couple were divorced.

Louella moved to Miami and looked after

Bobby Joe by day, but she had to leave him each evening to do bar or waitressing work. She would later admit that he suffered during these impoverished years. They were so poor that they would share a bed throughout his childhood, an increasingly inappropriate thing to do as the boy matured.

On other nights, his mother would bring a man to her bed, in which case Bobby Joe was told to sleep on the settee, from where he could hear them coupling. Some of these men were unkind to him, and he was increasingly full of hate.

When he was seven, his parents remarried but it was an off-and-on relationship and Louella continued to spend much of her time in Miami. That same year, Bobby Joe ran in front of a car and was badly injured; he was left with a deformed jaw and teeth. School bullies made fun of his strange appearance and he often returned home in tears. Although he had an IQ of 118, well above average, he had little concentration and performed badly at school. Later, he would have an operation to remove excess flesh from his chest as a genetic disorder had caused him to grow almost female-like breasts. Desperately unhappy, he took to torturing neighbourhood animals and began to fantasise about hurting humans, especially girls.

Meanwhile, in a desperate bid to make more money, his mother took a bar job that required her to dress in provocative outfits. The growing boy found this embarrassing and often pleaded with her to cover up, but the sexy clothes earned her more tips and increased her ability to attract new boyfriends – men that she continued to bring home.

Teenage romance

At thirteen, Bobby Joe met Cynthia, who was also from a broken home, and they became inseparable; he now stayed at her house whenever possible and was able to sleep apart from his mother. The couple dated for the next six years, during which time Bobby Joe was expelled from school for poor performance, became an electrician and joined the army. In January 1974, he and Cynthia married and she went to live with him at the air force base in Florida.

In March, he was out speeding on his motorcycle when it was hit by a car. He was left unconscious with a fractured skull, had shoulder injuries and almost lost a leg. In time, he recovered from most of his injuries, but the blow to the head left him with an overwhelming sex drive, so strong that the hospital nurses noticed that he was masturbating four or five times a day. This almost-manic lust was also infused with an equally overwhelming rage.

In August, he was released from the hospital and came home to Cynthia, who found that Bobby Joe had become sexually obsessive and now demanded intercourse at least twice a day. Within months he was discharged from the army on medical grounds so now had endless time to fuel his sexual fantasies. During this period he also used high levels of amphetamines.

Later that year, he was arrested in Dade County, when the daughter of an officer alleged that he had raped her, but the charge was later reduced and he was put on probation. His female probation officer found him very difficult to help as it was clear that he had problems being around women, but he moved to Tampa, was given a male officer, and was perfectly civil to him.

By late 1974, Cynthia had given birth to the couple's first child, a son, and Bobby Joe was paying his way through college, studying to become a radiologist. The couple had frequent arguments about money and he began to hit her. She promptly hit him back. The following year they had a second child, a daughter, but the situation was far from happy. The Longs moved house frequently and seemed to be perpetually dissatisfied.

The still-sexually frustrated Bobby Joe read the newspaper one day and realised that answering the classified ads would give him access to strangers, some of whom would be women. He began to answer such ads, showing up at the house pretending that he wanted to buy the goods for sale, then raping the woman if he found that she was alone.

The paramedic

The rapist continued to study Radiology at college during the day, but also did X-ray related work in the local hospital's radiology department at night. In the autumn of 1979, he graduated with an associate degree in X-ray technology. That November, he started work as an X-ray technician at a hospital in Miami Beach. He often made passes at the nurses and would grab them whenever possible. Some of the patients also found his manner disturbing and, the following year, he was dismissed. In the same time frame, Cynthia filed for divorce.

In 1981, police arrested him for making obscene phone calls to a twelve-year-old girl, and he was sentenced to two days in jail and six months' probation.

Domestic violence

Bobby Joe rented a room in a flat with a woman, but, in October 1981, she went to the police and said that he had raped her. A fortnight later, he viciously attacked her. When he was eventually found guilty, he inundated the legal system with complaints until he was given a new trial.

In January of 1982, he went home to live with his parents, who were back in West Virginia. One night, the couple were ambushed by two men, who tied them up at gunpoint and stole their possessions. Bobby Joe watched the mugging through a crack in his bedroom door. He consoled them that night, but ignored them on many other nights and was clearly restless and unhappy. He trained as a diver but couldn't find a diving job and was clinically depressed.

Further medical work

In February 1983, Bobby Joe's spirits rose when he was given a position as an X-ray technician at a hospital in Huntingdon. His employers were impressed with him, as was one of his female co-workers, whom he dated for a couple of weeks. Unfortunately, his lust overwhelmed him again and he began to tell female patients to strip, even when their particular X-ray didn't require this. He was fired within the month.

By the summer, Bobby Joe had found a technician's post at a hospital in Florida. He was only required to work weekends, which gave him ample time to answer classified ads during the day and rape the luckless women who answered the door. He began to date a nurse who was a born-again Christian and she persuaded him to go to church. (His maternal grandmother was a devout Baptist so he was familiar with religious belief systems.) He regularly gave her expensive jewellery that he had taken from the women he attacked.

Numerous rapes

On 6th March 1984, Bobby Joe called at a house that was for sale in Port Richey and, when a 21-year old woman answered the door, he forced her into the bedroom at gunpoint, tied her up and covered her eyes with surgical tape. He insisted that she fellate him, then he cut off her clothes, gagged her and tied her to the bed before raping her. He explored the property, identifying valuables, raped her again, and then fled with her jewellery and silverware. It's possible that he raped over a hundred women in this way; goods from numerous houses would later be found in his home but some of their owners couldn't be traced and others appeared to be too embarrassed to admit being victimised.

Murder unpunished

On 27th March 1984, the serial rapist picked up a twenty-year-old woman, Artis Wick, in Tampa. Known to hitchhike, she had left her apartment to buy cigarettes. Bobby Joe bound, raped and strangled her. (It would be nine months before her skeleton was found and he was never charged with this crime.) At the end of the month, he left his job without giving any notice, but continued to give his girlfriend necklaces and rings.

The following month he abducted a woman in her car, forcing her to drive at gunpoint. Realising that she would probably die if she drove to his preferred destination, she deliberately crashed the vehicle. He was arrested and scheduled to attend court later that year.

The first known murder

On 10th May 1984, Bobby Joe picked up a beautiful young Asian woman, Ngeun Thi Long, who was trying to hitch a lift home. It was sheer coincidence that she and her killer shared the same surname. She probably introduced herself by the Western name that she tended to use, Lana Long. The high-spirited twenty-year-old had worked as a go-go dancer but had plans to study Art at university. Her friendly manner and fit body ensured that she found it easy to get lifts.

She got into the amicable-looking Bobby Joe's car and he drove her to a wooded area and forced her to strip. He tied her up and drove to an even more secluded area where he placed her on her stomach, raped and beat her. During the rape, he strangled her to death with a rope. Afterwards, he posed the body, pulling her legs apart so violently that he tore some of her ligaments.

Three days later, two teenage boys found her decomposing corpse in a pasture and contacted police. Detectives found red fibres on the twenty-year-old's lifeless body, probably from the carpet in the killer's car. The field also included tyre tracks but, other than that, they had no clues.

Another rape

A fortnight after murdering Lana, Bobby Joe answered a classified ad where the advertiser was selling bedroom furniture. He went to the house in Palm Harbor, ascertained that the woman who showed him the furniture was home alone, and then hit her, tied her up and raped her. He also stole her jewellery.

The second known murder

On 26th May, Bobby Joe struck again, picking up former beauty queen Michelle Denise Simms on the Tampa Strip, the red light district in Florida where he found most of his victims. The 22-year-old had a cocaine habit, which she financed through prostitution. Bobby Joe posed as a punter, then stripped and bound her in his car. He drove her to a field and viciously raped her, but she put up such a fight when he attempted to strangle her that he finished her off with a knife, slashing through her jugular. He also used the blade to cut her face. After the murder, he threw her clothes around the field and left her wearing just her earrings and an anklet. It's likely that he stopped for refreshments as he apparently left an empty beer bottle at her feet. Michelle's body was discovered by a horrified construction worker the following day.

When police again found red fibres and tyre tracks at the scene they called in the FBI, who confirmed that this was the same killer. The bureau also found semen stains that showed A and B blood types, plus a head hair from a Caucasian male.

Another rape

Three days after he'd murdered Michelle Simms, the killer answered a classified ad in Pinellas County and raped the female house owner before making off with her jewellery, but his unhealthy lust wasn't sated for long.

The third known murder

On 8th June, he noticed 22-year-old Elizabeth Loudenbeck, a shy factory worker, who was out for a walk. Although she didn't normally accept lifts from strangers, she was taken in by Bobby Joe's good looks and superficially gentle manner, but within minutes of getting into the car, he'd produced a knife and told her to undress. Bobby Joe raped her in the car, drove to an orange grove in Brandon and sodomised her before making her put her clothes back on. After strangling her with a rope, he dumped her body underneath some shrubs. Finding her Cashline card and PIN number in her purse, he emptied her bank account. It was over a fortnight before her decomposing body was discovered and, as she was clothed and unbound (unusually, Bobby Joe had taken the rope with him), her murder was not initially linked to that of Ngeun and Michelle. Later, the FBI found the same red fibres on the corpse that had been found on the previous two victims, and realised that the killer had struck again.

The medic from hell

A week later, Bobby Joe started a new job as an X-ray technician at Tampa General Hospital. Now he could again feast his eyes on women as they undressed for mammograms. In the same time frame, he went to court for the attempted abduction of the woman who had crashed her car in a desperate bid to outwit him. Incredibly, he was only given probation and ordered to pay $1,500 for the damage to her car.

Another brutal rape

That summer, Bobby Joe went to Miami on holiday and picked up a prostitute, raping her and taking photographs of her degradation. He left her naked, beaten and shell-shocked, miles away from home.

The fourth known murder

On 27th September 1984, the X-ray technician was sacked. Co-workers later said that he was good at his job but that he sexually harassed the female staff and insisted on talking about sex to the male staff. He told one colleague that he 'liked bad girls and enjoyed fucking them in the ass.'

Three days after he lost his job, Bobby Joe offered a lift to eighteen-year-old Chanel Devon Williams. Using the same approach he'd taken with his previous victims, he drove her to a remote location – in this instance, a cattle ranch – where he tied, beat, sodomised and partially strangled her. Chanel struggled so valiantly that he finished her off with a gunshot to the head. A week later, her naked body was found and police again identified the red fibres found in the previous murders, yet they still had no idea who the serial killer was.

The fifth known murder

Later that autumn, on 7th October 1984, Bobby Joe killed again, picking up a prostitute called Kimberly Kyle Hopps, who offered him sex for $30. He took her to a darkened area under a bridge, where she was stripped and raped like his previous victims, although he strangled her with her own collar instead of using his trademark rope. He threw her corpse into a ditch but it wasn't found until the end of the month.

The sixth known murder

Bobby Joe claimed his next victim less than a week later, picking up 28-year-old Karen Beth Drinsfriend. Karen had good looks, a high IQ and a rampant drug addiction. She had spent time in jail for everything from grand larceny to heroin possession and her baby had been given to foster parents. Now she made a living from selling herself.

Karen asked Bobby Joe for the exact amount she needed for a fix: $47, and he readily agreed to the price. However, once she was in the car, he turned on her and tied her up. He drove her to a remote location and dragged her from the car, raping her from behind whilst jerking on the rope around her neck. After he'd finished strangling her, he posed the body, pushing up her sweatshirt to expose her breasts.

The seventh known murder

The X-ray technician's next victim, at the end of October, was eighteen-year-old Virginia Lee Johnson, who'd turned to prostitution to support her drug addiction. After she got into Bobby Joe's car, he tied her up and took her to a lonely field where he raped and strangled her, using a heavy shoelace and a fabric rope. When her corpse was found after a fortnight in the sun, it was badly decomposed and had been partially eaten by animals. She was eventually identified by the heart-shaped pendant she often wore and by her dental records. By this stage, each kill was giving Bobby Joe less of a buzz than the previous one, and he was soon out hunting again.

A terrifying abduction

On 3rd November, at 2.30 a.m., he was cruising around when he spotted a beautiful seventeen-year-old, Lisa McVey, cycling home from her late-night job at a restaurant. Bobby Joe parked, pulled her from her bike and manhandled her into his car at gunpoint, where he forced her to strip and fellate him. During this act he warned her to keep her eyes closed. Afterwards, he blindfolded her and drove around for a while, before taking her to his apartment, where he attempted to sodomise her and then raped her. Bobby Joe showered with the petrified teenager before blow-drying her hair and complimenting her on her appearance. He took her into his bed and raped her repeatedly throughout the night and during the following day.

During this period, he seemed to want the girlfriend experience, asking her about her job and her family. He made her a sandwich and urged her to rest. Twenty-six hours later, he drove her to a parking lot, told her how much he liked her, and released her. The shell-shocked teenager removed the blindfold, got her bearings and ran home to her father, who called the police.

Lisa had seen Bobby Joe in the moments before he first blindfolded her and was able to give a good description. She also described his voice, his build, his age range, car and gun. She was able to describe his apartment in similar detail, as he'd removed the blindfold after she'd been there for a while, though he warned her not to look at him.

By now, police from several forces had established a task force to catch the killer. They were convinced that their quarry was the man who had abducted and raped Lisa McVey.

The eighth known murder

After setting Lisa free, the X-ray technician resumed his murder spree; Kim Marie Swann, aged twenty-one, was his penultimate murder victim. Bobby Joe picked up the pretty blonde dancer in early

November and subjected her to a terrible ordeal, putting a leash around her neck and repeatedly tightening and loosening it. Rope burns on her body testified to the desperate struggle she'd put up. He beat her about the head and she lost control of her bowels, after which he lost the desire to have sex with her. When she was dead, he forced her legs as far apart as they would go. Her body was found on 12th November, and the police estimated that she'd been dead for two or three days.

The ninth known murder

In late November, the body of 21-year-old Vicky Elliot was found and she became known as Bobby Joe's last murder victim, but she had actually been murdered much earlier, on 7th September. That night, the radiographer saw the pretty and petite young woman walking to her late-night shift at a coffee shop. A nice girl and a reliable employee, she was about to start training as a paramedic and was an asset to society. Bobby Joe offered her a lift and she accepted, keen to get out of the dark and the cold.

Within minutes, Bobby Joe attempted to tie her up but, she pulled a pair of scissors from her bag and managed to stab him in the chest.

Enraged, he beat and tied, raped and strangled her before dumping her body on a dirt road. As a further act of humiliation, he pushed the scissors up her vagina until they lodged in her pelvic cavity.

Arrested

Meanwhile, detectives were closing in on the unemployed X-ray technician. In mid-November 1984, they followed a red car that fitted the description Lisa McVey had given them. They pulled Bobby Joe Long over and asked to see his driving licence, casually explaining that they were looking for a robber. Now that they knew his name and address, they let him go.

They were able to ascertain that Bobby Joe had made a withdrawal from a cash machine at the time and place where Lisa McVey had been dumped, and that he had a record for abduction and rape. Armed with this information, they quickly secured a search warrant and FBI assistance. As he left the cinema the following afternoon, they arrested him.

Detectives talked to Bobby Joe about his earlier rape conviction and the recent abduction of Lisa McVey, and the killer soon admitted taking and raping the teenager. He said that she was a good kid and that he regretted attacking her. He was comfortable talking about this case – after all, he'd been arrested for rape before and this had had limited consequences – but when the police began to question him about the murders he looked dismayed and said that he might want legal help. Detectives told him that fibres from his stair carpet had been found on several of the bodies, as had his hair, adding that he was an intelligent man who must know that this was overwhelming evidence. Flattered by their words – and perhaps tired of killing – he confessed to everything. He also told them where to find Vicky Elliot's corpse.

Later that night, he phoned his ex-wife Cynthia and told her about the murders, asking her to tell their children that he was dead.

Trial

Awaiting trial, the serial killer was examined by six mental health experts who all agreed that he had known what he was doing, that he was sane. However, they found that there was mental illness on both sides of his family and believed that his unhealthy upbringing, coupled with later head injuries, had left him at an increased risk of committing antisocial acts against women. That said, he was found competent to stand trial.

Meanwhile, Bobby Joe began to sketch out a plan to escape from prison, and, when this was discovered, he was moved to a higher-security cell.

In April 1985, he went to court in Pascoe County for the New Port Richey rape; the jury took under forty minutes to find him guilty. Later that month, he was convicted of Virginia Lee Johnson's murder and sentenced to death by electrocution. He remained unmoved.

A month later, he agreed to a plea bargain, whereby he'd serve a minimum of fifty years for seven of the murders, rather than go to court for all eight murders, but the death penalty was still on the table, as the murder of Michelle Simms would go through to the sentencing phase. Always one to play devil's advocate, Bobby Joe repeatedly changed his mind about the plea bargain and also changed his legal team.

To everyone's surprise, his new attorney introduced Bobby Joe's confession to his first murder, that of Artis Wick. He said that Bobby Joe's traumatic childhood and head injuries meant that he was a sick man, out of control, and was not responsible for his actions. The jury remained unconvinced and, on 25th July 1986, voted that he be put to death by electrocution for the murder of Michelle Simms.

Games people play

Since sentencing, Bobby Joe Long has issued appeals from Florida's Death Row and managed to get a retrial for the Virginia Lee Johnson case, arguing that he hadn't been given an attorney. He was again found guilty in 1988 and sentenced to death, but this was overturned in 1992. He was tried yet again in 1994 and again sentenced to death, each appeal being heard at the taxpayer's expense.

Bobby Joe went on to do the same thing with the Michelle Simms case, and was given a new sentencing hearing. The death sentence was upheld but has yet to be carried out. Although he took the lives of at least ten women – and ruined the lives of his numerous rape victims – Bobby Joe Long is still alive today.

PART EIGHT

WHY THEY KILL

Why does a respected paramedic turn into a crazed, lust-driven killer? What makes a nurse suddenly start murdering the children in her care? The final section looks at the various motives of lethal doctors and other healthcare staff and includes an illuminating interview with a forensic psychologist.

35 Typologies of Medical Killers

As the previous chapters have delineated, doctors, nurses and paramedics kill for a wide variety of motives. In some instances, the killer has two or even three motives – Kristin Gilbert, for example, enjoyed the excitement when a patient went into cardiac arrest but also used a sudden death on the ward as an excuse to leave work early to be with her new lover. There may also have been a Munchausen's syndrome by proxy element to some of her murders. Most healthcare killers were motivated by one or more of the following:

Hero on the ward

This type of killer – often a nurse – gains a sense of purpose and satisfaction through reviving a seriously ill patient. This would be laudable if they hadn't originally caused the life-threatening attack by administering a near-fatal medicinal dose. Such medics invariably suffer from one or more personality disorders and don't really care if the patient dies prematurely or in great pain – but, if he or she lives, they will bask in the compliments from their fellow nurses and will often boast about their medical knowledge and years of experience.

Munchausen's syndrome by proxy

Again, these killers are often nurses. Most start off as Munchausen's syndrome sufferers, harming themselves in a myriad of ways in order to get treatment from their doctor or the outpatient department of the local hospital. When one hospital becomes suspicious, they will move to another in a different area. Upon becoming nurses or paramedics, they will transfer their obsession with injury and symptoms onto their hapless patients, with sometimes fatal results.

Thrill killers

Such murderers get a charge from watching someone die. They invariably discuss the deaths at length with other nurses or even try to engage the bereaved relatives in conversation. Such killers sometimes insist on accompanying the corpse to the mortuary. They often become addicted to murder – and to fooling the authorities – and kill with increasing frequency.

Lust killers

Most of the lust killers in this book were male doctors, powerful men who thought that they should have anything – and anyone – they wanted. Their female victims either died of a bad reaction to the date rape drug that had been callously administered to them, or were killed after threatening to report the attacker to the authorities. Anthony Joyner, a modest diet technician at a nursing home, was the exception. He was also atypical in that he clearly meant to kill his patients (after all, he had the option of letting one rape victim go after she fled to the bathroom), despite his claims that they died of accidental suffocation during the rapes.

Resentment

There have been several instances of male nurses who hated elderly women and were incensed at having to bathe and clothe them. They expressed their hostility verbally before starting their killing sprees. These men really wanted to be doctors and resented having to do basic bodily care as opposed to administering medication and checking on the patient's vital signs. As such, they would have felt a level of resentment towards anyone who required help with feeding and washing tasks.

Financial gain

Several of the medics profiled in this book would have benefited from insurance policies if they'd eluded a murder charge. Despite their high earnings, some had amassed considerable debt. Though the main motive was financial, the murders also provided secondary satisfaction by getting rid of a prodigal son or unwanted wife.

Other motives

Katherine Ramsland, who teaches forensic psychology at DeSales University, Pennsylvania, has identified more complex motives, from perverted compassion (euthanasia) to necrophilous voyeurism, where the medic holds values that makes him or her embrace death over life. She details those in her landmark book, *Inside the Minds of Healthcare Serial Killers*, which covers cases from 1910 to the present day.

In June 2009, I interviewed this criminologist and frequent contributor to Court TV's *Crime Library*, asking her to comment on notable cases and suggest why such killers remained at large for so long. My questions and her replies are preceded by our initials.

CAD: Charles Cullen features on the front of *Inside the Minds of Healthcare Serial Killers*. Is he the most prolific American healthcare killer that you've written about? If not, who claimed the most known victims? And what was his or her motivation? Here in Britain we have Harold Shipman, who appears to have broken all UK records.

KR: *Shipman currently holds the world's record for documented healthcare serial killers, I believe. The record in the US goes to Donald Harvey, since Cullen stopped short of his prediction by admitting to 29 murders and 6 attempts. He's probably responsible for more, and he did claim the number could be as high as 40, but he stopped talking, and so far, nothing more has been proven. Harvey made extravagant claims for his victim count, reportedly into the 80s, but he pleaded guilty to one manslaughter and 36 murders over the course of 18 years – he even kept a journal. A few were acquaintances, not patients. Harvey killed for petty reasons as well as mercy, he says. One man he just didn't like; another he killed out of revenge. And then there were the acquaintances he poisoned with arsenic who had just annoyed him. His attorney thought Harvey was projecting his depression onto his potential victims – a psychologist said the same thing about Cullen – but Harvey also dabbled in the occult, so it's possible he was experimenting with substances as well. Often, there's more than a single motive for these crimes, especially if the killer has years to evolve. Some even begin with mercy and then find they like the sense of power. They change as people, and so, they change as killers.*

CAD: Many homicidal nurses have a history of suicide attempts yet hospitals hesitate to fire them. Have you any thoughts on why hospitals don't sack staff who are so obviously mentally ill?

KR: *It's difficult to fire someone, especially for mental health reasons, because the institution could be sued. They would have to prove that*

*the person's condition negatively affected his
or her work performance, and that's tough
to do. Many of those who were mentally
ill actually had good work records. Each
situation is different, however, so I hesitate
to say that there's a general reason for this
that covers all, or even most cases. I can't
really speak for hospital administrators.*

CAD: Similarly, homicidal healthcare staff often
have a medical history which points to
Munchausen's syndrome. Why, do you
think, is this so frequently overlooked?

KR: *It's easy in retrospect, after a suspect's
defence is pieced together, to acknowledge
the pattern of this illness, but it's not as easy
to recognise it in a day-to-day situation.
Munchausen patients are typically secretive
about their manipulations. They want
attention, but they don't want anyone to
know how they're faking their illness to get
it. That's a difficult diagnosis to make, along
with its associated diagnosis Munchausen's
syndrome by proxy, and it requires seeing
the patterns over the course of a person's
medical history. However, I might also
say that just because someone is claiming
to suffer from either of these conditions
doesn't make it true; this particular*

syndrome has become an effective way for females to mitigate their guilt and get a lesser sentence.

CAD: I note that various healthcare killers, including Charles Cullen, Bev Allitt and Kristen Gilbert, had a history of hurting and killing animals. Is there scope for hospitals to approach 'prevention of cruelty to animals' organisations and ask if a prospective nurse has a record of animal maltreatment? Or does the US legal system prohibit this?

KR: *Often, this comes out only during an investigation, but cruelty to animals is rarely on the record anywhere, especially if it occurred when the suspect was a kid. Cullen, for example, was cited for neglect of his dog, but he did spare the dog when he prepared to fill his apartment with poisonous fumes during a suicide attempt. So is he cruel or kind? The neglect could have been the result of his depression or debt, so it wouldn't necessarily be defined as aggressive cruelty. This is a difficult issue, because cruelty to animals does not necessarily evolve into murder or serial killing; second, plenty of serial killers have not been cruel to animals; and third, just because there's a record of animal cruelty with some agency, what can you really do with it? It's not predictive; it's only valuable as part of the whole package when pondering criminal behaviour. To identify a possible healthcare serial killer requires a number of different 'red flag' behaviours, collectively, not just one, and others are easier to connect to murder.*

But back to your question: think of all the many things an employer has to do to process a person's application to be a nurse. Checking all possible animal welfare agencies for a violation would be both burdensome and impossible. You'd have to find a practical and efficient way to do this, as well as ensure that it's not an invasion of privacy, and even then, you couldn't prove anything about the person's work competence with an animal cruelty charge. Things we know in retrospect are not necessarily practical ways to identify a person's capacity for murder. I think there are more obvious behavioural signals that can be documented.

CAD: I take your point – Britain is a much smaller country so animal cruelty and child cruelty agencies are beginning to communicate, as there's an increasing awareness that the man who is taken to court for torturing his dog is often also abusing his wife and children.

Can we do anything, in both the US and the UK, to spot psychopathy in healthcare workers? I'm thinking of Chante Mallard, whose actions after accidentally hitting a man with her car were sociopathic. Had she shown such psychopathy in her everyday life or in her work as a nurse's aid?

KR: *I wouldn't call it psychopathic, since I think she was scared, high, and hysterical that night. She apologised over and over to her dying victim, and then gave control of the situation to others as she lay crying on the floor. This incident had not been a cold-blooded, calculated or predatory act. Granted, she talked about it later in a way that gave the impression that she had no remorse, but from the testimony of others involved on that night, she would not fit the cold and manipulative behaviour of a psychopath.*

Mallard did have a problem with substance abuse and she also tried to destroy evidence, but she wasn't out to target helpless people for her own benefit. It was intentional murder only in that she did not get the help her victim needed, but that was more about being emotionally unable to cope with the consequences of hitting someone while driving under the influence. I would call her behaviour unprincipled, ignorant and immature, like a self-centred adolescent, but I wouldn't say she was psychopathic. At her trial, no one said that she was generally an uncaring or cruel person.

CAD: So what do you make of smooth talkers such as nurse Orville Lynn Majors, who was so plausible when he appeared on *The Montel Williams Show* that he convinced a top criminologist of his innocence? Do such men – and women – ever end up in a quasi-medical role in prison or are they automatically forbidden from working in the prison sick bay?

KR: *It depends on their skill in convincing others of their competence, as well as on the type of prison they're in and the personalities of the people they encounter. Edmund Kemper, who killed both of his grandparents when he was 15, ended up giving the psychiatric assessments to other troubled kids in psychiatric detention because he figured out how to pass them himself. Once released, he killed a number of young women before murdering his mother. Truthfully, it really depends on how much sympathy they're able to garner or how well they can win the trust of the warden. Some can, others can't. As years pass, their crimes have less impact and their present manipulative charm has more. In addition, if prisons are understaffed, they might be allowed into supervised situations that tap their training and skills. I didn't study these people in prison, so I can't say with authority what would happen, but I can see how it might be possible.*

CAD: Finally, is there anything else that you particularly want to say about healthcare serial killers or the hospitals which employ them?

KR: *Too often, hospitals have protected themselves first, patients second. Over and over, these killers have been allowed to drift from one hospital to another, fired or let go under a cloud of suspicion, but rarely brought to justice until after incriminating evidence has reached alarming levels. While there is no distinct psychological type, there are important signals: secretive behaviour, missing medications associated with the person, a preference for the shift with the least number of co-workers or supervisors, statistically significant spikes in deaths on a certain person's shift – especially unexpected deaths, moving around from one facility to another and spotty past work records can be troublesome signals.*

Once such a person is investigated, other signals have frequently popped up. Notably, there are several suspicious incidents associated with this person at different institutions, some of the lethal substance was found in the person's home or on the person for no good reason, and there are inconsistencies in their statements when questioned. In addition, they often have lied about something on their application or in their job interview. While none of these items is in itself sufficient to place someone under suspicion, a number of them together in constellation should be sufficiently alarming to colleagues and facility administrators to keep closer watch for solid evidence of lethal behaviour.

Acknowledgements

My grateful thanks go to criminologist Katherine Ramsland for her invaluable contribution to the Typologies of Medical Killers chapter. Katherine teaches Forensic Psychology at DeSales University and is the author of more than twenty crime books including *The Human Predator: A Historical Chronicle of Serial Murder and Forensic Investigation, The Devil's Dozen: How Cutting-edge Forensics Took Down 12 Notorious Serial Killers, Inside the Minds of Serial Killers* and *The Criminal Mind.*

I'm equally indebted to Dr David A Holmes, senior lecturer at the Department of Psychology and Social Care at Manchester Metropolitan University, author of *The Essence of Abnormal Psychology* and a contributor to numerous forensic research projects and crime documentaries.

I'd also like to acknowledge Caitlin Rother's

contribution to the Kristin Rossum profile. Caitlin, an investigative journalist and Pulitzer Prize nominee, attended most of Rossum's trial and wrote an incisive book, *Poisoned Love*, about this complex case. She is also the author of *Body Parts*, which examines the inner world of serial killer Wayne Adam Ford, and *Twisted Triangle*, a former FBI agent's account of her ex-husband's attempt to take her life.

Select Bibliography

Begg, Paul and Fido, Martin *Great Crimes and Trials of the Twentieth Century* Carlton/Simon & Schuster, 1993.

Black, Ray and Hall, Alan and Smyth, Frank *Real Crime Scene Investigations* Abbeydale Press, 2006.

Distel, Dave and Distel, Lynn *Hunt to Kill* Pinnacle, 2005.

Fanning, Diane *Under the Knife* St Martin's Paperbacks, 2007.

Flowers, Anna *Bound to Die* Pinnacle, 1995.

Furneaux, Rupert *Famous Criminal Cases 6* Odhams Press Ltd, 1960.

Glatt, John *Twisted* St Martin's Paperbacks, 2003.

Goldacre, Ben *Bad Science* Fourth Estate, 2008.

Griffiths, John *Fatal Prescription* Hancock House, 1995.

Heilbroner, David *Death Benefit* Warner Books, 1994.

Kennedy, Ludovic *10 Rillington Place* Victor Gollancz, 1971.

Kidd-Hewitt, David *Bristol & Bath Whodunnit?* Countryside Books, 2007.

Linedecker, Clifford and Burt, William *Nurses Who Kill* Pinnacle Books, 1990.

Long, Stephen *Out of Control* St Martin's Paperbacks, 2004.

McCrary, Gregg *The Unknown Darkness* HarperCollins, 2003.

Noel, Barbara with Watterson, Kathryn *You Must Be Dreaming* Poseidon Press, 1992.

Peters, Carole *Harold Shipman: Mind Set on Murder* Sevenoaks, 2005.

Phelps, William M *Perfect Poison* Pinnacle, 2003.

Ramsland, Katherine *Inside the Minds of Healthcare Serial Killers* Praeger, 2007.

Rosencrance, Linda *Murder at Morses Pond* Pinnacle, 2004.

Rother, Caitlin *Poisoned Love* Pinnacle, 2005.

Rule, Ann *Bitter Harvest* Little, Brown & Company, 1998.

Thernstrom, Melanie *Halfway Heaven* Virago, 1998.

Van Over, Raymond *A Father's Rage* Pinnacle, 1998.

Whitlock, Chuck *Mediscams* Renaissance Books, 2001.

Whittle, Brian and Ritchie, Jean *Prescription for Murder* Warner Books, 2000.

Filmography

The Angel of Death Real Crime Series, True North Productions. Broadcast ITV1, December 2008.

Born to Kill? (Harold Shipman). Broadcast Sky Three, December 2008.

World's Worst Sex Change Surgeon (John Ronald Brown). Broadcast Channel Four, April 2007.

Index

S

T

U